Child of a King

The Biblical Doctrine of Sonship

For

Fiona
Lindsay and Andrew

Child of a King

Mark G. Johnston

Christian Focus

© Mark Johnston
ISBN 1 85792 188 7
Published in 1997 by Christian Focus Publications, Geanies House,
Fearn, Ross-shire, IV20 1TW, Great Britain

Cover design by Donna Macleod

Printed in Great Britain by
The Guernsey Press Co Ltd, Vale, Guernsey, Channel Islands.

Contents

The doctrine of adoption as defined by the
Westminster Assembly of divines

THE CONFESSION OF FAITH

12. Adoption

All those that are justified, God vouchsafeth, in and for his only Son Jesus Christ, to make partakers of the grace of adoption (Eph. 1:5. Gal. 4:4, 5): by which they are taken into the number, and enjoy the liberties and privileges of the children of God (Rom. 8:17; John 1:12); have his name put upon them (Jer. 14:9; 2 Cor. 6:18; Rev. 3:12), receive the Spirit of adoption (Rom. 8:15); have access to the throne of grace with boldness (Eph. 3:12. Rom. 5:2); are enabled to cry, Abba, Father (Gal. 4:6); are pitied (Psalm 103:13); protected (Prov. 14:26), provided for (Matt. 6:30, 32; 1 Pet. 5:7), and chastened by him as by a father (Heb. 12:6); yet never cast off (Lam. 3:31), but sealed to the day of redemption (Eph. 4:30), and inherit the promises (Heb. 6:12), as heirs of everlasting salvation (1 Pet. 1:3, 4; Heb. 1:14).

THE LARGER CATECHISM

74. What is adoption

Adoption is an act of the free grace of God (1 John 3:1), in and for his only Son Jesus Chrit (Eph. 1:5; Gal. 4:4-5), whereby all those that are justified are received into the number of his children (John 1:12), have his name put upon them (2 Cor. 6:18; Rev. 3:12), the Spirit of his Son given to them (Gal. 4:6), are under his fatherly care and dispensations (Psalm 103:13; Prov. 14:26; Matt. 6:32), admitted to all the liberties and privileges of the sons of God, made heirs of the promises, and fellow-heirs with Christ in glory (Heb. 6:12; Rom. 8:17).

THE SHORTER CATECHISM

34. What is adoption?

Adoption is an act of God's free grace (1 John 3:1), whereby we are received into the number – and have a right to all the privileges – of the sons of God (John 1:12; Rom. 8:17).

Preface

Out of all the influences which come to bear upon us in life and shape what we are and how we develop, none are more powerful and evocative than those found in family relationships. Some people grow up in good and happy family circles with the very best of relationships, for others the experience of family is the opposite. In either case the moulding effect of family life is dramatic. As human beings we are in very essence family creatures.

It was a great discovery for me in my understanding of the Christian faith and life to realise how God relates to us in those very categories. The good news of his salvation and what it means to experience that salvation are described in terms of relationship lost and relationship regained. The Christian life is not some abstract theory or dry set of rules, it is nothing short of a living, meaningful relationship with the living, personal God. The Fatherhood of God and its related themes in Scripture open a truly thrilling window on our understanding of God's message to the world. It is with the desire to give vent to the thrill of these truths that, however hesitantly and imperfectly, I wrote this book.

I am indebted to Sinclair Ferguson, friend and mentor, who first opened that window for me during a chapel address in Westminster Seminary in 1984. His writings have stirred me to explore this theme more fully for myself.

My thanks are due as well to Malcolm Maclean of Christian Focus Publications for the invitation to write this book and share these thoughts with a wider public. My deepest appreciation, however, is reserved for my own family, to whom these pages are dedicated, for all that they mean to me and for all that God has taught us together.

Where there are quotations from the Bible, they are taken from *The New King James Version* (Thomas Nelson Publishers; Nashville), 1994, unless otherwise stated.

The desire that lies behind this book quite simply is that those who pick it up and read it might come to discover and appreciate the wonder of what it means to be a child of God and what it cost God to establish that relationship.

Introduction

One of the recurring tragedies in the history of the Christian church and its preaching of the gospel is its ability to make God seem more remote than he really is. Instead of 'preaching the gospel', the church has made the mistake of preaching *about* the gospel and so made it appear abstract and distant. The effect of this on both believer and seeker alike has been to rob God's message of the warmth and vitality he has invested in it, leaving it dry and scholastic. The most effective antidote to this is to look afresh not only at *what* God reveals of himself in his Word, but also *how* he reveals it.

The Bible describes salvation from many different and complementary perspectives. Only when we hold all these perspectives together in balance do we get a full picture of what it means to be a Christian. If we emphasise one perspective at the expense of others, we end up with a distorted picture of the far-reaching realities of God's saving work. It seems rather strange, therefore, that Scripture's emphasis on the Fatherhood of God and the sonship (a generic term embracing both male and female) of his redeemed children has been significantly overlooked by evangelical writers.

The Confession of Faith and two Catechisms, which were the main documents to emerge from the Westminster Assembly, acknowledged the significance of this strand

of biblical revelation by including separate statements on the doctrine of Adoption and its significance. Other credal statements have tended to subsume the treatment of adoption into statements on justification. Apart from that, there was a flurry of reformed interest in the subject in Scottish circles in the middle of the last century,[1] but this passed and received little attention in the wider evangelical world either then or since. More recently there has been an indication of renewed interest in this aspect of Christian truth both at a scholarly and a popular level.[2] One can only hope this signals the beginnings of a wider concern to highlight these truths for the benefit of all.

The value of this God-given perspective on his truth is manifold. It provides a handle on the gospel to which ordinary people can relate readily. Whereas it is true to say that it is the Holy Spirit who enables people to grasp God's message in a way which will lead them to salvation, it is also true to say that God has made himself known by coming down to the level of the humanity he has purposed to save. John Calvin described it as being like a nursing mother speaking to the child in her arms in baby-language, because that is the only communication to which the infant can relate.

The practical importance of this is perhaps greater than we imagine. The world in which we live is being secularised rapidly. God is receding from the collective awareness of the up-and-coming generations, making it increasingly difficult to present the message about God in terms that people can appreciate. So, if God himself has provided an angle on his truth which strikes a chord in the hearts of people as he has made them, then surely we

need to exploit that for his glory and for the spread of his Kingdom.

The family language which pervades Scripture as it speaks about God, his people and the relationship which exists between them, displays the warmth of the gospel in a striking way. It is not the presentation of a system, a philosophy, or even a ritualistic religion; it is a personal God speaking to men, women and children, made in his own image, and calling them into the most intimate relationship with himself.

The force of this dimension of the gospel is perhaps felt even more keenly in an age like ours, where, at least in the western world, stable family life is rapidly coming apart at the seams. It could be argued that the disintegration of the traditional family presents an obstacle to biblical teaching about the family of God because it is a concept which is far-removed from contemporary norms. In reality the opposite is true. What people have been deprived of, and yet crave in terms of stable family relationships, is being offered to them in the gospel. Even in extreme situations, where experience of a human father has involved abuse and pain, the stark contrast of God's Fatherhood is thrown into much sharper relief. Everything a human father ought to be and yet has failed to be – and infinitely more besides – can be found and experienced in fellowship with God.

Indeed, when the eternal proportions of these truths are brought into focus, they highlight for all the fact that the disappointments, failures and limitations of our human families can be put right only when we are brought into God's everlasting family.

The intention of this little volume is to introduce and explore the amazing truth that to be a Christian is to be a member of God's family. It is a discovery which has life-transforming implications for those who are coming to God for the first time. Also, it is a discovery which has life-enriching consequences for those who are Christians but for whom spiritual experience has become jaded because they have failed to appreciate the fullness of what they are and have in Jesus Christ. The sheer wonder of it all is summed up in these lines by Hattie E Buell:

My Father is rich in houses and lands,
He holdeth the wealth of the world in his hands!
Of rubies and diamonds, of silver and gold,
His coffers are full, he has riches untold.

I'm the child of a King, the child of a King!
With Jesus my Saviour, I'm the child of a King.

My Father's own Son, the Saviour of men,
Once wandered o'er earth as the poorest of them;
But now he is reigning for ever on high,
And will give me a home in heav'n by and by.

I once was an outcast stranger on earth,
A sinner by choice, and an alien by birth!
But I've been adopted, my name's written down,
An heir to a mansion, a robe, and a crown.

A tent or a cottage, why should I care?
They're building a palace for me over there!
Though exiled from home, yet still I may sing:
All glory to God, I'm the child of a King!

There can be no greater joy, pleasure or privilege, in this world or the next, than to know with certainty that you are 'the child of a King'.

1

Born to be God's Children

It no longer seems to be fashionable to discuss and debate the great questions of the meaning of life, yet they still remain. Even if they are not being articulated in a reasoned form, every generation wants to know who we are, where we came from, why we are here and where we are going. The *crie de coeur* emanating through contemporary music, drama and art is the plea to resolve a modern identity crisis. If this longed-for resolution is going to come, we must attempt to untangle the threads of the issue and begin to see it from a perspective that is rapidly being forgotten: the viewpoint of God's Word. There, and there alone, do we find a view of humanity that explains its origins, meaning and purpose in life, and so restores the dignity that has been denied so many people in so many places.

God left out

It may be wrong to make sweeping generalisations, but it is becoming the accepted norm in the western world to try to understand everything without reference to God. Society is more and more self-consciously secular. That does not necessarily mean that it is atheistic, rather that God, if there is a God, is disregarded for all practical

intents and purposes. Modern man is agnostic.

The theory of evolution is taught uncritically in schools and universities, broadcast with apparent unwavering certainty on nature programmes on television, and enjoys a measure of general acceptance as fact which is not warranted by the scientific evidence given in its support. Its popular appeal (despite the disagreement on particular details within the scientific community) stems from its being a respectable way of removing God from the picture in an attempt to understand the world and universe. More to the point, it purports to allow us as human beings to try to discover an identity for ourselves that has no reference to God.

The implications of this approach are enormous. Closing the door on an absolute Being effectively excludes all sense of an absolute morality, a clear distinction between truth and falsehood and any idea of the need to distinguish between religions. Hence, not surprisingly, we find growing confusion over these kinds of issues. In the midst of the pluralism that has come to characterise so many societies, there is a real struggle over the consequences of life with no fixed code of conduct and no clear view of God. Communities are full of the casualties of this mindset: those who sincerely and eagerly tried this new lifestyle only to discover the pain it inflicts when it doesn't work.

Despite the confusion and pain, there is still, it seems, a deep-seated awareness that there is more to life than the popular pundits are telling us. Somewhere in our common psychology there is the sense of needing to belong and to relate. This sense expresses itself in the evocative associations of 'home' in our instinct and understanding.

Even in those for whom the experiences of home life have been negative, there is still an instinct for what 'home' ought to be, regardless of what it was for them. The question is, what to make of this?

A bridge into God's Word

We find a fascinating incident related in the Bible where there is an encounter in Athens between Paul, the great missionary apostle, and the men of the Areopagus, an elite group of philosophers and religious thinkers (Acts 17.16-34). What is interesting is the fact that these men had no prior knowledge of the God of the Bible and Paul is faced with the problem of showing that he is the true God and that they need, not only to relate to him, but to respond to his message through Jesus Christ. He seeks to bridge the gulf between the world of thought and experience with which they were familiar and the world of God's Word by means of this basic human instinct. The sense that not only is there a God, but that somehow human beings can reach out and relate to him (Acts 17.27).

Paul quotes Epimenedes, a Cretan poet who lived in the seventh century BC whose work the Areopagites would have known, saying, 'for we are also his offspring' (Acts 17.28). This poet was a pagan who knew nothing of Paul's God, or of what is said about that God as Creator of the world, universe and everything they contain. Yet Paul is able to pick up on this line of poetry and open it up in the light of the account of God and creation in Genesis to show how true it is and what important implications it holds for the entire human race.

Paul in effect was appealing to a fact about God that is universally known through General Revelation, that is, what God has revealed of himself generally in the created order as opposed to specially in the Bible (see, e.g., Rom. 1.18-20). It is something which is implanted into the human consciousness and understanding by God himself. Elsewhere Paul speaks about how much is known about God through what he has revealed in creation (Acts 14.17; Rom. 1.20), enough to make people aware of God's existence, his character and human accountability to him, but not enough to save them. Here Paul highlights one particular facet of that God-consciousness: the sense that the relationship of the human family to God is one of children to their father.

This is not the only place in the Bible where this thought is advanced. In Luke's account of the genealogy of Jesus, he traces his ancestry back to Adam and rounds it off with the words, '...the son of Adam, ... the son of God' (Luke 3.38). In other words, although Adam came into existence, not by ordinary procreation, but by the direct creative action of God, his relationship with God was that of son. Again, when Jesus tells the parable of the prodigal son (Luke 15.11-32), the lost son (who represents those who are lost in sin) returns to his father, who is still his father despite the son's prodigality. While in the far country he says, 'I will arise and go to *my father* and will say to him, "*Father...*"' (Luke 15.18). Certainly, as he goes on to indicate in the next verse, he no longer deserves to be called a son, because of his rebellious behaviour, but the relationship still stands.

Looking at man's relationship with God in these terms

is not without its dangers. It would be all too easy to argue that if every human being sustains a child-father relationship with God, then all human beings will ultimately enjoy the blessings of God's family. This was the line of reasoning followed by liberal theologians during the nineteenth century as they explored the Bible's teaching on the fatherhood of God. They argued from the universal fatherhood of God and the universal brotherhood of man to the universal experience of redemption. Not surprisingly such logic found little quarter in evangelical circles and so this thinking was vigorously rejected by evangelical scholars, most notably by the Scottish theologian, Robert Candlish.[3] He argued that 'sonship', in the narrow redemptive sense, was something different from what Paul was describing as 'sonship' in the sense of being God's creation. Candlish chose to view the relationship between God and man which existed in the Garden of Eden from the legal perspective of subject to Sovereign, while viewing the Christian's relationship with God through adoption as being of the same order as the relationship between Jesus and the Father.

Another notable evangelical theologian of that time, J.L. Girardeau, a Southern Presbyterian in America, opposed the view of Candlish. He saw it as being not only permissible but more faithful to Scripture to retain the concept of created sonship, while still allowing for its having a different sense from adoptive sonship in redemption.[4] Approaching the issue from this angle allows us to hold on to both the sense and the language of the biblical passages cited. In so doing, the impact of the gospel on the mind and heart of those who hear is, if anything, intensified.

The uniqueness of man

When we approach the Bible's handling of human identity with this in mind, we see, in a quite remarkable way, the utter uniqueness of the human race. The key truth is, of course, the account of God's creation of man in the first two chapters of Genesis. Even though there were certain similarities between human beings and animals (they were all made on the sixth day of creation), there is a profound distinction between these two groups. The distinction stems from what man is and how God made him.

God said, prior to the creation of man, 'Let us make man in Our image, according to Our likeness...' (Gen. 1.26). These words are indicative of man's uniqueness in the entire created order. It is as though there is a special sitting of the divine Council to consider this critical juncture in the creative process. This is endorsed by the unusual way in which the creation of man is effected. Every other facet of the created world and universe came into being at the behest of God's spoken word: 'Then God said, "Let there be..." ... and there was...' see, e.g., (Gen. 1.3,6,9). When it comes to the creation of man, however, it is not divine fiat which brings him into existence, but divine action. God takes the dust of the earth, fashions it into a human form, then personally breathes life into this body (Gen. 2.7). Everything about the creation of humanity says that it is special.

Later on in the Bible, especially in the Psalms, we see further reflection on this fact and mystery, with the associated response of praise and thanksgiving to God. Human dignity is acknowledged in that man is made 'a little lower than the angels' and is 'crowned with glory

and honour' (Psalm 8.5). The complexity of our human make-up is pondered in that we are said to be 'fearfully and wonderfully made' (Psalm 139.14).

This majestic uniqueness accorded to the human race stems supremely from the fact that man is made in the image of God, he bears the mark of his Creator in his very being. In that sense, there is a unique relationship between man and his Maker – there is, if you like, a family resemblance which bears out the existence of this special bond. Since God in his glorious being is not one Person in isolation, but a Trinity of Persons in eternal inter-relationship, so those who bear his image on earth do not exist as isolated beings, either as individuals, or as a race. Again, the fact that God, as it were, 'got his hands dirty' in the making of man says something about a unique involvement with the human race which is not shared with any other species or genus.

The bottom line is that man was created to exist in fellowship with God and to enjoy a relationship with him of the most intimate sort. The time-honoured opening statement of *The Westminster Shorter Catechism* captures it well when it says that man's chief end is not only 'to glorify God' (as subject to sovereign), but 'to enjoy him forever' (as child with father).

The original outworking of that relationship is seen in the Garden of Eden. God placed his children in the best of what is already the very best – it is hard to conceive of superlatives in the context of what is supreme in its entirety! Eden clearly is meant to symbolise an earthly sanctuary where the localised presence of God could be enjoyed in a special way. What makes it Paradise is not its contents,

but the One who graces it with his presence. When Adam and Eve hide from God after their disobedience (Gen. 3.8) the suggestion seems to be that it had been habitual for them both to walk with God 'in the cool of the day'. When that time came on that particular day, they could not bear the thought of facing him. If that is the case, then the daily evening walk of man with Maker is a glorious image of the child-with-father relationship. A relationship which involves a sharing of all that is deepest, best and most precious. The picture we are given in the first two chapters of Genesis of the first human couple is one of perfect well-being in every sense. What holds it together in the experience of Adam and Eve is the fact that they are able to enjoy the world in which they live in fellowship with God.

Such a view of *homo sapiens* is quite contrary to that which prevails in the scientific and popular textbooks of our day. There man is seen as a lonely figure desperately struggling to survive in a hostile environment among loveless creatures. It is a view which only serves to reinforce man's sense of alienation and isolation, not only on the planet, but within his own race. The efforts of scientists to analyse the world and man's place in it are, of necessity, confined to the material order of reality. It is beyond the scope of science to delve into the spiritual realm. (This is borne out by the difficulty experienced by pure evolutionists in trying to account for morality and spirituality in human beings.) Thus they end up with a picture of perceived reality which falls short of true reality and experience.

It is quite correct to acknowledge that there are

remarkable similarities, anatomically, between humans and animals, but that does not warrant the assertion, so popular today, that man is merely a 'human animal' and no more. By trying to explain our humanity through relating it downwards to the animal kingdom, scientists effectively strip the race of its dignity. When people are told over and over again that they are nothing more than exalted animals, it is inevitable that sooner or later they will begin behaving like animals in their social and moral conduct. The principle of 'survival of the fittest' has a cruel edge to it.

It is only when the human race is understood by means of upward relationship, as we find in Scripture, that we see its true dignity and worth. The psalmist gives a breathtaking description of the exalted position of man when he says:

> You have made him a little lower than the angels. And You have crowned him with glory and honour. You have made him to have dominion over the works of Your hands; You have put all things under his feet... (Psalm 8.5-6).

Human beings were created to be God's children.

The broken image

When Adam and Eve chose to disobey God (Gen. 3.1-7) they brought upon themselves, and indeed upon the entire race, consequences of devastating proportions. God had warned them in advance what would happen if they disregarded his simple injunction concerning the tree of the knowledge of good and evil: 'In the day that you eat of

it you shall surely die' (Gen. 2.17). The threat was fulfilled, as God had said, in the moment of disobedience. Death was experienced, not in the physical sense of soul being severed from body, but in the spiritual sense of man being cut off from God. In that instant the spiritual umbilical cord, binding man in perfect fellowship with God, was cut.

That did not mean, however, that every last vestige of the prior relationship was eradicated. The image of God in man was marred, but not destroyed completely. Man did not cease to be the child of God in the sense of his being God's special creation, but did become a child in rebellion. As such, he came under the Father's wrath and condemnation (Gen. 3.16-24), but did not lose the latent awareness that his true identity was somehow bound up with relating to God.

Someone has expressed it in terms of the tension, or *angst*, which has, since that point in time, existed within the human psyche. A tension of wanting, at one and the same time, to run from God as the Judge of all the earth, and yet to run to him as the father we were created to enjoy. Perhaps the words of Augustine of Hippo provide the best expression of what this means in practice: 'Lord, you have made us for yourself and we have no rest until we find our rest in you.'

The key to the human predicament

This idea of restlessness in the soul of man provides the explanation for many of the problems that are experienced in life. If we take it to be the case that God created the

human race originally with the intent of its enjoying a unique relationship with him and that we are only truly 'at home', or at rest, when we are in that relationship, then outside that relationship we can never know lasting inward peace.

One peculiar way in which the yearning for this peace expresses itself is the desire for 'home'. It is not just the lost and frightened child who sobs, 'I want to go home'; many an adult, out of their depth and in turmoil in life's problems, has quietly groaned, 'I want to go home.' What they mean by that is, quite simply, that they want to be in the place where they are secure, accepted and at peace. Our human homes and families can go a long way in meeting that need, but even the best fail to go far enough to satisfy truly. That is because even the best are not impregnable. They are all prone to assault from the pressures of life, sickness and, ultimately and inevitably, death.

There have and always will be other 'homes' where people try to find the kind of security their soul craves. For one person it will be a job – a vocation, a profession where he or she finds fulfilment and reaps rewards. For another it will be the 'home' of a supportive and caring circle of friends – a group which provides a sense of belonging and being valued. For someone else it will be religion. For another, the little world he or she has constructed and feel they own.

It is not hard to see how all these different homes are doomed, eventually, to collapse and fail those who built their hopes and aspirations upon them. Jobs are lost, friends disperse, possessions decay and go out of fashion.

Even then, the instinct for 'home' lingers on. In the worst scenario, where all is lost, and a person is living on the street, that deeply ingrained instinct remains. Those who work among the homeless of big cities frequently find, to their bemusement, that these people 'of no fixed abode' have their own railway arch, or shop doorway to which they go each evening, they seek the company of the same group of people every day, and are grieved when either of these securities is lost. In the midst of their 'home-lessness' they desperately try to create a home.

For those who have plumbed the depths of destitution, the longing for a home is expressed in seeking refuge in alcohol or drugs, the search for a home becomes escapism, an effort to anaesthetise themselves and find a temporary rest through artificial means.

At the heart of it all lies a spiritual problem. Man, whatever the state of his bank balance, or size of his house, is spiritually a vagrant. In the same way as Cain, after his sin against Abel, was doomed to be 'a vagrant and a wanderer on the earth' (Gen. 4.12, NASB), so all sinners wander aimlessly through life until God finds them and they find God. Hence the gloomy verdict on life without God in Ecclesiastes: 'All is vanity' (Ecc. 1.2). The apostle Paul states this sombre reality even more starkly in his comment on the futile thinking and darkened understanding of those who do not know God (Eph. 4.17-18). The Creator's intent, built in to the very fabric of what we are, is that only when we are part of God's family do we discover the full potential of our humanity.

Back to the Areopagus

Going back to Paul's encounter with the men of the Areopagus in Athens, it was precisely this point he was making in his presentation of the gospel. His starting point was to appeal to the general awareness of God and the common need to relate to him. It was this sense of God, even though blurred and confused by sin, which lay behind the amazing display of religion in the Athenian agora where this meeting was taking place. Paul had already commented on the bewildering array of shrines and deities on display and in particular on the rather peculiar altar with the inscription, 'To the Unknown God' (Acts 17.22-23). He goes on to blow away the blurred images of general revelation in the light of God's clear and special revelation in his Word and in his Son. He is able to proclaim to them with confidence the truth about the God they worship in ignorance (Acts 17.23)

The interesting thing in what he says is that the general sense of God, which these men apparently acknowledged, gives grounds for accountability to God (Acts 17.30-31). If it is the case that God has made the entire human race, then a relationship exists between them. The race is ultimately and logically answerable to the God who made it.

That in itself is hardly 'good news'. Since the race is guilty of rebellion against God, then it can expect only the wrath and condemnation of the God it has offended. But the point needs to be established. Paul had to impress upon his hearers the fact that they were responsible, not ultimately to themselves, or to their imaginary gods, but to the true and living God. The writer to the Hebrews expresses the same thought in slightly different language

when he describes God as the One 'to whom we must give account' (Heb. 4.13).

The effect of this sobering truth on the runaway sinner is not unlike the effect of the news to a runaway child that he is being taken home to his father. While 'on the run' it is quite possible to suppress all thought of being answerable to someone else. The sense of 'freedom', artificial though it is, can be quite exhilarating. But when reality is faced and the relationship (which never ceased to exist) is brought home, then the consequences are felt. The thought of standing before the God who has made us and against whom we have rebelled is terrifying indeed. But before there can be a genuine restoration of the lost relationship, there has to be an honest facing of the facts. The sense of need has to be established before the needs themselves can be either addressed properly, or met.

So the message of accountability and judgement for Paul is but the precursor to the liberating news he has come to proclaim in Athens. As he opens God's Word to these people, it must wound them before it can heal them. The 'hook' upon which the apostle hangs the gospel is the universal awareness that God exists, that he has been offended by human behaviour, and that his favour somehow needs to be sought if his judgement is to be avoided. Before the good news of God's salvation in Jesus Christ can be declared, the bad news about what we are as fallen creatures has to be faced.

A fact for every generation

These truths about the origins of the human race and the implications arising from them about God and our relationship to him are crucial for each generation if they are to appreciate and benefit from God's message to the world.

Successive generations have tried desperately to wriggle free from any sense of obligation to God, or need to listen to his gospel. This has been the case from the very beginning. Paul describes it in terms of people 'who suppress the truth in unrighteousness' (Rom. 1.18). That is, people who deliberately and self-consciously attempt to evade what is self-evidently true. It is the story of so many lives. Put in contemporary language, it is the protest that 'Your God has no claim on me.' In our pluralistic society the God of the Bible is submerged (much as he was in the Athenian agora) in the crowded market-place of the deities of the world. He is reduced to 'one among many', with no more significance than any. But God does not allow us to go down that route. Even if a person was never to open a Bible, never to listen to a sermon, never to meet a Christian, they would still be conscious of God and of his claim on their lives.

Paul uses very powerful language in Romans to describe man's efforts to dodge the issues. When he speaks about those who 'suppress' the truth, he uses a word which conveys the clinical wilfulness which is involved. It is not unlike the action of a murderer who holds his victim's head under water until the kicking and struggling have stopped. So man's quest to write God out of history and personal experience becomes inevitably the murder of Truth.

When people face the truth about themselves and about God they see a sad and frightening picture. Yes, there is a father-child relationship there, but it is a relationship turned sour. Instead of being the sons and daughters of his love and favour, as we were meant to be, in our sinful fallen state we have become 'sons of disobedience' (Eph. 2.2; 5.6) and 'children of wrath' (Eph. 2.3). As Girardeau has put it:

> Sinners and devils are sons in revolt – sons disinherited, excommunicated, reprobated, but still sons, under the indestructible obligation of nature to render filial obedience to God.[5]

For such, the prospect of meeting God one day is not of a happy family reunion, but of stubborn recalcitrants brought home to 'face the music'.

Happily, that is not the end of the story, nor does it exhaust the significance of the unique relationship between God and the human race brought about through creation. It has implications, not merely for the anger of God, but also for his love. It is the glorious truth that lies behind one of the best known verses in the Bible: 'For God so loved the world...' (John 3.16). The love of God expressed there is not the detached love of a distant observer, but the heartfelt love of One who has been uniquely bound up with this world. It is the love of One who has been spurned by those he loved, yet truly longs for a restoration of the relationship that once was (Hosea 11.1-8).

The whole purpose of God's sending his 'only-begotten Son' into the world, the focus of his great plan of salvation,

is that Jesus might be 'the firstborn among many brethren' (Rom. 8.29) and that he might bring 'many sons to glory' (Heb. 2.10). The very essence of redemption is the restoration of God's family that was lost at the fall. As the Bible opens up and develops the many dimensions of this theme, the wonder of what God has done through Christ becomes even more evident, and our appreciation of what it means to be in Christ unspeakably enriched. And that is where we must go from here.

2

Numbered Among God's Children

We have looked at the original state of humanity as created by God and in perfect child-father relationship with him in the Garden of Eden. We have seen how that relationship was broken and its benefits lost when Adam and Eve rebelled against God and brought sin and disobedience into the world. We have considered also, in outline form, God's plan of redemption – his intention, not merely to restore man to the position which was lost through the fall, but to raise him to new heights of fellowship, privilege and blessing through his own Son, Jesus Christ.

Now we must go on to consider the outworking of that plan in history and in God's dealings with his people. Although we may be inclined to rush straight into the New Testament to see the salvation of God in all its fullness, we need to begin in the Old Testament. As we trace the unfolding drama of redemption through its pages we see how there, even at that early stage of God's dealings with people, the threads of fatherhood and sonship are plain and prominent in God's saving intentions. As we follow those threads we are led inexorably into the New Testament, to the exposition of these truths about salvation that is not only heard from the lips of Christ, but embodied in his incarnate life. Those self-same truths are then opened

up more fully in the apostolic preaching and teaching of later New Testament revelation.

When *The Westminster Shorter Catechism*, with its characteristic pithiness of expression, summarises the meaning of adoption, it describes it as a gracious act of God 'whereby we are received into the number ... of the sons of God'.[6] Let us start by seeing how God graciously began to number people among his children from the very beginning of Old Testament times.

Mercy in the midst of judgement

In order to trace the roots of this Old Testament teaching, we need to go back once more to Eden where several details are worth noting. In the cataclysmic plunge from the paradise of God's pristine world (Gen. 1.31) to the paradise lost of world-turned-wilderness (Gen. 3.24), it is the Fatherhood of God which brings his identity as Creator and Judge into perspective.

There has always been a tendency to question why it was necessary for God to place any restrictions upon Adam and Eve in the Garden as he so obviously did when he forbade them to eat the fruit of the tree of the knowledge of good and evil (Gen. 2.16-17). Was that prohibition not a blot on the landscape of a perfect world? That may be so were it the case that man was intended to be a free agent in the fullest sense of the word, but he was not. As we have seen already, man was created for fellowship with God, and his enjoyment of God's world was contingent upon his sustained fellowship with God and submission to his will. As the *Westminster Shorter Catechism* reminds

us, 'the good things of life' can be enjoyed only when they have God's 'blessing with them',[7] that is, in communion with him. Thus the prohibition concerning the tree is not so much restrictive as protective, designed to preserve right relationships between man and his environment in the wider context of a right relationship between man and his Maker. It is but an early expression of God's fatherly love. The father who warns his child about bad company or dangerous places is not the kill-joy his child might perceive him to be, but a loving father who wants only the best for his child. Thus God's warning about death being the consequence of disobedience (Gen. 2.17) is intended to preserve the paradise in which our first parents lived and ensure their enjoyment of it.

The little gloss at the end of that chapter where it says, 'And they were both naked, the man and his wife, and were not ashamed' (Gen. 2.25), is much more profound than it may seem. It describes not merely two people perfectly at ease in each other's presence, but two people perfectly at ease in God's presence even though they knew their lives to be transparent before him. But all of this was to change.

Adam and Eve allowed themselves to be taken in by the serpent's subtle lies about God and his words (Gen. 3.1-6). They consciously ignored the warning they had been given and deliberately took the fruit they had been forbidden to eat. They rebelled. The immediate consequence of their rebellion was shame (Gen. 3.7). In total contrast to their shamelessness in the previous chapter, they were now hiding from God, desperately trying to conceal themselves from his gaze. They knew full well

what they had done and they did not need to be told what they deserved. They lived in dread of their next encounter with God. But it was precisely that encounter which was to say so much about God both to them and to their posterity.

Someone has said, and rightly so, that the fact Adam and Eve lived to hear God's voice again was of enormous significance for them in terms of what God is like. We are perhaps too quick to home in on the words of condemnation which God utters in the verses that follow (Gen. 3.9-19). That God allows his voice to be heard at all is the earliest example of Jeremiah's comment, 'through the LORD's mercies we are not consumed...' (Lam. 3.22). God could have executed his immediate retribution upon his children, but in his grace and mercy, they lived to hear him speak and learn his intentions for them and for his world.

There was condemnation, for them and for the devil, but there was grace as well: the promise of deliverance. The outstanding truth of God's pronouncement, which reverberates throughout the entirety of Scripture, is the promise of One who would 'bruise' the head of the serpent (Gen. 3.15). Into the darkness of God's words of curse and condemnation shone the light of God's promise of deliverance and restoration. The wrong which had been done that day with all its horrendous ramifications would ultimately and eternally be put to right by the One that God would send. Another abiding truth about the nature and character of God was being revealed. He is the One who 'in wrath remembers mercy' (Hab. 3.2). There was mercy in the midst of judgement.

The first three chapters of Genesis constitute a roller-

coaster ride of truth for those who come to it for the first time. We are taken up to the very pinnacle of perfection and bliss in the world and garden God made, plunged over the precipice of despair as we see humanity bring ruin upon creation, only to be caught in the arms of God's mercy and given hope that keeps us reading! The scene is set for everything else that will follow as God's revelation unfolds.

Israel, my Son

It is fascinating to see that though the contours of the father-child relationship are discernible in Eden, the language of such a relationship is absent. It is applied retrospectively (Luke 3.38), but not overtly in the perfect environment where we might expect it to belong naturally. Instead, it is as God's saving purposes begin to unfold that we discover those God calls to himself being described in filial terms.

The first place where God speaks of his relationship with his people in the intimate language of the family is in the call of Moses. There Moses is told to tell Pharaoh on God's behalf, 'Israel is my son, my firstborn' (Exod. 4.22). It was particularly significant that God should speak of the relationship in those terms at that time because the bond between Israel and their God was under severe strain. The Israelites were in slavery to the Egyptians and their cry went up to God (Exod. 2.23). It seems that there had been a measure of spiritual decline among the Israelites during their years in Egypt, and the hardship they experienced under the Pharaoh was in some sense being used in a disciplinary way by God. It is as though they

need to be brought to an end of themselves before they turn to God for help. Their underlying fear of having been forgotten by God is highlighted in the fact that God says on no less than three occasions that he has seen their plight and has not forgotten his covenant bond with them (Exod. 2.24-25; 3.7-9, 15-17). God sought to reassure his people by reminding them of his covenant love and faithfulness.

Thus he speaks of the relationship between them in language that will take to new heights their understanding of what it meant to be in covenant with God. It was more than a bond between king and vassal, it was that of father to child. When the children are in the depths of despair, the Father comes to them in all his tenderness and reminds them of what he is to them and what they are to him.

The implications of that relationship are brought out later on in the Exodus as Moses expounds God's Law to the Israelites and pinpoints their deepest motivation to obey it. 'You are the children of the LORD your God; you shall not cut yourselves nor shave the front of your head for the dead...' (Deut. 14.1). There was far more than bare legal obligation as the motivating force behind Israel's obedience, rather a relationship with God as Father which only they enjoyed.

To appreciate the dimensions of this Old Testament relationship between God and his people, we need to go into the realm of God's covenant dealings with them. There we see that there is a fatherhood of God in relationship to his covenant people which is distinct from his fatherhood in relationship to the human race and the entire created order. Paul clarifies it for us when he speaks of the unique

privileges enjoyed by the Israelites, 'to whom pertain the adoption, the glory, the covenants, the giving of the law, the service of God, and the promises' (Rom. 9.4). To dispel the notion that he is speaking merely of some kind of ethnic or national privilege, he goes on to draw a further distinction within national Israel, saying that it is not the natural descendants of Abraham who enjoy this relationship with God, but rather 'the children of the promise' (Rom. 9.8). In other words, those who had been brought into saving fellowship with God through his gracious promise of redemption.

God's covenant in its various Old Testament manifestations repeatedly marked the convergence of the love of God and the law of God. It was invariably undergirded by God's sovereign, saving provision for his people: with Noah (Gen. 8.21-22), Abraham (Gen. 12.1-3), Moses (Exod. 20.1-2), David (2 Sam. 7.8-9) and the anticipation of the New Covenant (Jer. 31.33-34). The paternal dimension of God's saving grace in his covenant comes out strongly in later prophetic appeals when his covenant people are straying from him (Isa. 1.1-2; Jer. 31.9, 20). The relationship between God and his people was always grounded on his saving initiative and action and its benefits received through faith (See, e.g., Gen. 15.6). But side by side with God's covenant provision were his covenant stipulations, the obedience he required of his redeemed children (Gen. 9.1-7; 17.1; Exod. 20.3-17; 2 Sam. 7.14; Jer. 31.33). The two were never to be seen at odds with one another, but rather as two essential aspects of divine fatherhood.

There was always a tendency among God's people in

Old Testament times to emphasise the legal aspect of the divine-human relationship at the expense of the gracious element on which it rested. Hence God's frequent repetition of his desire for religion which emanated from a renewed heart rather than mere formalism (Isa. 29.13); but for God's part, it was never conceived of as something cold and legalistic. The intensity of God's feeling for his people who are in covenant with him is brought out over and over again in the prophets as God appeals to his erring people through them. Nowhere is this more striking than in the prophecy of Hosea, where the disobedience of Israel is portrayed in terms of the heart-rending pain inflicted through adultery. As the prophet is grieved through his wife's marital unfaithfulness, so God is grieved by the disobedience of the people he has loved and provided for. It is in the context of that prophecy that we again find God speaking in terms of a father-child relationship.

'When Israel was a child, I loved him, and out of Egypt I called my son...I led them with cords of human kindness, with ties of love; I lifted the yoke from their neck and bent down to feed them' (Hosea 11.1, 4).

There is a depth to God's fatherly love which can never be plumbed, even in the glimpses seen before the coming of Christ.

This is not to say that Israel had no knowledge or appreciation of God as Father at all. The psalmist was able to relate to God with some awareness of his fatherly love and compassion (Psalms 27.10; 103.13), and the writer of Proverbs was conscious of a paternal dimension to the discipline God administers to his people (Prov. 3.12).

Then when God's people find themselves at their spiritual extremities there is a child-like consciousness which causes them to cry out to God, not as a remote deity, but as Father (Isa. 63.16; 64.8; Jer. 3.4). There was some sense of God's being Father to those who clung to him by faith – an awareness which was based on God's revelation, not merely an innate God-consciousness – but it was embryonic and in need of development.

Paul explains Israel's failure to appreciate the dimensions of this relationship as being the result of God's people in the Old Testament being spiritual minors (Gal. 3.23-25).[8] That is, because God's revelation of himself and of his redemptive purposes was not yet complete, it was necessary to place his people under the oversight of the law. He uses an illustration from everyday life in the ancient world where a child, who may well have had good parents and stood to gain a fine inheritance, was put under the care of a slave known as a *paedogogos*. The task of this slave was not simply to ensure the child was educated, but also to act as a guardian. Inevitably, when the child was small this meant putting all kinds of 'fences' around him to impose an external discipline until the child grew to maturity and was able to exercise self discipline out of a deeper appreciation of the relationship with his father. So Paul would go on to show how the 'coming of age' of the people of God coincided with the climax of his revelation in Jesus Christ.

Son of God and Son of Man

Jesus Christ is the pinnacle of God's revelation to the world. He is 'the Word' (John 1.1), the embodiment in human flesh of God's message: incarnate revelation. He is the enfleshment of all that God is (Col. 2.9) and so is able to say, 'He who has seen me has seen the Father' (John 14.9). He is also God's last word, the climax of all that God has to say to the human race and creation he has made (Heb. 1.1-3). There is an ultimacy about God's revelation in Jesus Christ which is simply unsurpassable. It should not surprise us, then, that in Jesus, God's message about how he relates to his people and how they relate to him comes into its sharpest focus.

The mystery of the Person of Jesus Christ himself brings us straight into the realm of the relationship between humanity and deity. When Jesus was conceived in the womb of the virgin Mary, he became something which previously he was not. The Creator took to himself the flesh and nature of the creature. He was made like all other human beings in every way, with the exception of sin (Heb. 2.14, 17; 4.15). The One who was eternally the only begotten Son of God in the moment of his conception became the Son of Man. He humbled himself, not by subtraction, but by addition (Phil. 2.7). As we are introduced to Jesus of Nazareth, it becomes clear that there is simply no-one else like him. He is truly unique. In him uniquely and perfectly deity relates to humanity and humanity relates to deity.

In the Person of Jesus Christ the gulf between Creator and creature is bridged. The nature of deity and the nature of humanity are essentially different. They cannot relate

to each other in natural terms, but in Jesus the true point of contact is established.

It is also true to say that in Jesus Christ alone the yawning chasm is spanned between a God who is just and holy and a race which is sinful and guilty. He, 'the man Christ Jesus', is 'the only mediator between God and men' (1 Tim. 2.5).

The whole point of the incarnation is the bringing together of God and man. The shape, form and outcome of the incarnation demonstrate that God and man are brought together in Father-child relationship.

This was a breath-taking discovery for the disciples. Their Master was not only rocking the foundations of the religious establishment of their day, but was encouraging them to do so as well. He was telling them to adopt a completely new pattern in their prayers in their approach to God. Instead of not daring to take the name of God upon their lips, they were to come and address him as 'Our Father...' (Matt. 6.9). When thinking of God and his provision for his people's needs they were not to think of him as a detached and distant deity, but as the Father who knows his children's needs (Matt. 6.8). In terms of their practical personal relationship with God, Jesus was teaching his disciples to 'boldly go where no man had gone before'.

In taking his disciples into this new realm of under-standing of the relationship between God and men, Jesus was careful to preserve the line which distinguishes his unique relationship to God as 'the only begotten of the Father' from their relationship with God which can come about only through their being in him. When preparing

for his departure from his disciples to return to his Father in heaven, he says to Mary Magdalene, 'I am ascending to My Father and your Father, and to My God and your God' (John 20.17). They shared the same relationship with God, but in a different way: Jesus by virtue of what he was from all eternity; the disciples by virtue of what they were in Christ.

Jesus revolutionised the way God's people thought about God, not only as he explicitly taught them how they were to relate to God in the New Testament era he ushered in, but also through how they understood Jesus himself and came to appreciate the relationship with God that was secured exclusively through him. Both elements come together in Jesus' well-known statement on the eve of his crucifixion: 'I am the way, the truth and the life. No-one comes to the Father, except through Me' (John 14.6). Speaking as the One who himself is both God and man, he points to himself as the only way by which men may come to God and enjoy communion with him of the most intimate kind.

Such revolutionary revelation is then brought centre-stage in the remainder of the New Testament as the apostles open up more fully this amazing truth which has blossomed in Jesus Christ.

God's extravagant love

The apostle John, as he writes the Gospel which bears his name, seems to refer to himself under the pseudonym 'the disciple whom Jesus loved' (John 13.23; 19.26; 20.2; 21.7, 20). And it is that New Testament writer who makes much

of the Father-child relationship of God to his people as the most extravagant expression of his love. When he says in his first epistle, 'Behold what manner of love the Father has bestowed on us, that we should be called the children of God...' (1 John 3.1), he is speaking about love that is off the Richter Scale of human experience. It is love that truly 'takes your breath away'.

It is almost as though this ageing saint grasps his readers by the ancient equivalent of their lapels, shakes them vigorously and says, 'Don't you realise what you are in Christ?' After years of theological cud-chewing (this letter was probably written late on in the first century AD) John was simply enraptured by the glory of this truth – God has made those who believe in his Son his children! 'Beloved [his form of address is the next best thing to red ink], now we are the children of God...' (1 John 3.2). Remember what you have become in Jesus and never forget what you will be one day when God has finished his work in your life.

Add it all together and it can be seen only as one thing: extravagant love. Love shown in the lengths to which God has gone to save his people: he sent his Son to be their Saviour. Love shown in the price which God had to pay in order to secure their redemption: he punished his own Son in the place of those who were his enemies and who deserved to be punished. Love shown in the heights to which God raised those who Christ actually saved: he brought them in to the intimate confines of his family and called them his own sons and daughters. It was the most uplifting reminder these people could have heard.

Again, the circumstances of those on the receiving end

of this circular letter which John was sending out had a
bearing on what they needed to hear. These were the
members of congregations which were bruised and
perplexed by persecution from without and the emergence
of heresy and schism from within. They might well have
been forgiven for feeling that they had somehow slipped
outside the orbit of God's loving embrace. Yet John
emphatically assures them that nothing could be further
from the truth.

His emphasis is upon the legal rights and entitlements
which a Christian has by virtue of his or her relationship
to Jesus Christ. These are very much to the fore from the
opening lines of his Gospel – a treatment of the coming of
Christ which not merely records the events of Christ's
coming, but reflects upon their significance. There he says,
'...as many as received him, to them he gave the right to
become the children of God' (John 1.12). Upon all who
came to trust in Jesus God conferred the status of sons.

It was a status which was inviolable. It could not be
shaken by circumstances or diminished by feelings and
failures. It was a relationship with God which is legally
established and upheld by the finished work of Christ.

It is not unreasonable to assume that John was building
on a theological foundation which had already been laid
by Paul and which, even by this relatively early stage in
church history, was common knowledge among God's
people. Paul had certainly been responsible for a more
technical treatment of the mechanics of being brought into
the family of God and the privileges associated with it.

In his letter to the Galatians (one of the earliest, possibly
even *the* earliest of Paul's letters[9]), the centre-piece of

Paul's message to these Christians who were being tempted to rely on their good works for acceptance with God, was his great statement about the status given to those who believe in Christ (Gal. 3.26-4.7). They were no longer slaves, but sons and heirs (Gal. 4.7).

Having explained the importance and significance of what it means to be justified by faith in Christ (Gal. 3.1-9), Paul goes on to highlight another dimension of this saving relationship with God, namely, adoption into God's family. The Judge who has justly acquitted the sinner now becomes the Father who takes him in to his home. No longer is he addressed, coldly and somewhat distantly, as 'Your Honour', but rather as *'Abba*, Father' (Rom. 8.15).

The whole thrust of what Paul is saying is that we are what we are in relation to God, not by looking to ourselves and what we have done, but by looking ever to Jesus and what he has done. The whole orientation of the Christian's life, by faith, is turned away from self to Jesus, not just at the beginning of their Christian experience, but as the on-going, daily reality of Christian experience. Paul has to chide the Galatian Christians because, having begun their relationship with God by looking to Jesus, they have tried to sustain that relationship by looking to themselves (Gal. 3.3). They have lost sight of the sheer wonder of what God has given to his people in and through his Son. As if it were not enough in itself for him to forgive their sins and accept them as righteous in his sight on the basis of the righteousness of Christ imputed to them, he goes way beyond that and receives them as his children.

It is all too easy for Christians of every generation to fall into the same trap as the Christians in Galatia and

those to whom John was writing and lose sight of what God has made them in fellowship with his Son. Whether it be the shame of personal sin, failure and inconsistency, or the pressures and difficulties of life which weigh so heavily upon us, the effect is the same; our eyes are taken off our Saviour and we begin to sink. Our confidence in God is shaken, our self-esteem begins to plummet and the joy of our salvation starts to feel like ancient history. There is no need for any Christian to have to go down that road at all. If the perspective of our faith is as it ought to be, then our spiritual eyes will ever be fixed on Jesus, the One who is the Author and the Finisher of faith (Heb. 12.1-3). But even when Christians do find themselves sucked into that kind of despair (as many of their predecessors have been), the antidote is the same: look again to Jesus. The effect will be to remind them what they are, not in themselves, but in union with Christ.

To be numbered among the children of God is the zenith of Christian experience. It means appreciating what we have become in Christ as the starting point from which we can go on to appreciate what we have received and what is yet in store for us in fellowship with him. As we begin to explore the various dimensions of this privileged state, we must begin by considering how a saving relationship with Jesus Christ brings us into a new relationship with each Person of the Godhead: Father, Son and Holy Spirit. Each makes a distinct contribution to shaping the character and blessing of the Christian life as life in the family of God.

3

My Father and My God

God has made himself known to his people in a multitude of ways throughout his Word. He is the Eternal God: the God who simply *is* (Exod. 3.14, cf. Gen. 21.33; Heb. 11.6), the One who always has been there and always will be there, 'from everlasting to everlasting ... God' (Psalm 90.2). He is the God of supreme might and power (Gen. 17.1), towering above the capabilities of every other professed deity (Isa. 44.9-11) and the combined capacities of the human race (Gen. 11.1-9). He is 'God Most High' (Gen. 14.19), the One who alone is worthy of praise and worship from his creatures. He is the sovereign Lord, the Judge of all the earth (Gen. 18.27, 25), the God who is in heaven and does whatever pleases him (Psalm 115.3). The revelation of God given in the Bible is overwhelming in its splendour and intensity. To try to gaze upon his glory in our natural state is as impossible as trying to gaze into the sun with unprotected eyes. We are told that those holy creatures which surround the throne of God in heaven must always cover their faces before him (Isa. 6.2) – the pure holiness of God is too much for them to contemplate directly.

It is not surprising, then, that in Old Testament times the overriding awareness of the 'otherness' of God filled people with the sense of it being impossible for them to

have direct fellowship with him. It was commonly believed that to see God meant inevitable death (Deut. 5.26). Hence the amazement of Manoah and his wife, the parents of Samson, when they met with God in the Person of the Angel of the Lord and survived (Judg. 13.22). Any kind of intimacy with God was alien to their thinking – even to the extent of being in the proximity of God's felt Presence.

Such thoughts about God were reinforced by the layout of the Tabernacle and Temple and the instructions which governed their use. The Presence of God was symbolically screened off in the Most Holy Place behind a heavy curtain (Exod. 26.31-35) – a room barred to human access apart from on the Day of Atonement when the High Priest would enter bearing the blood of sacrifice for the sins of the people, which he would sprinkle on the mercy seat on the ark of the covenant (Lev. 16.15-16). It was impossible to think of God, or of approaching him, lightly.

Such self-disclosure on God's part was not in any sense cruel or unkind. Rather he saw it as vital to impress upon the human race the reality of who he is and the seriousness of what it means to be in rebellion against him. He was making it clear that we cannot relate to God on the same plane as we relate to our fellow men. Only against the back-drop of God's majesty and glory can we appreciate the true dimensions of human need and helplessness and see the greatness of the salvation that God himself provides through his Son. It leads ultimately to a relationship which is cherished because it is seen for what it really is.

I remember once as a teenager setting out by myself to play a round of golf on a seaside course and being invited by an elderly couple to join them to make up a threesome.

I accepted the invitation happily and somewhat casually proceeded to play the game and chat as we went along. It was only when we reached the eighteenth green that the gentleman informed me that he was the Archbishop of Armagh – the Primate of all Ireland. Had I known that from the outset of play, my game, let alone my conversation as a mere teenager in such company, would not have been so casual or off-hand! Conversely, if I had known from the start what I came to know at the end, it would have made me more appreciative of the privilege that was mine as the game progressed.

Thus as God's relationship with his redeemed race begins to unfold from early times in biblical history, it is as though God is impressing upon his people the reality of who he is and the privilege of knowing him at all. Only then, as the relationship unfolds into more intimate fellowship, will privilege be grasped and treasured. The God who has revealed himself by 'the eighteenth green' of his unfolding revelation, is not only the God of all majesty and splendour, but the God of unfathomable love.

God is love

The well-known and often-quoted declaration that 'God is love' (1 John 4.8) has been trivialized in the minds of many today. This is true in part because the whole concept of what love is has been trivialized in our contemporary world. To be in love for the average person these days means to be conscious of their hormones stirring within them when in the company of someone who they find attractive. In an extreme sense this can be nothing more than naked lust – an overwhelming desire to be sexually

gratified by this other person. In a more respectable vein, it is being conscious of a personal chemistry that is consistently aroused by one other person. This grand delusion about the definition of love has been powerfully and dramatically popularised by the music and film industries of our day.

While it would be naïve and prudish to dismiss or discount these erotic and romantic elements of love, it is the suicide of love to regard it merely in these categories. Indeed, it is precisely because love, in the common perception, is nothing more than these things that it is increasingly robbed of true meaning and dignity. People quickly discover that it is as easy to fall out of love as it is to fall into it. Before there can be any true appreciation of a God who is love, there is an enormous meaning barrier which has to be crossed. Only then do we realise that this is actually a credit to God.

The blame for this trivialized view of God as love lies, not only in secular culture, but also in the Christian community. As a younger generation of Christians has allowed its mind-set to be shaped more than it should have by the world and its values (Rom. 12.1-2), its grasp of the depth of God's love has been impaired. This has surfaced perhaps more than anywhere else in the realm of popular songs and choruses. There are, of course, many expressions of praise in contemporary language which have retained a rich appreciation of the love of God, but, sadly, there are all too many others which have not. The lyrics are shallow and even where a generous spirit might say that deeper truth might be drawn from them, there is no-one there to guide the worshipper into it. The church as

much as the world needs a fresh confrontation with the contours and dimensions of God's love, described by Paul in all its height, depth, length and breadth (Eph. 3.18), to see it, not only as emanating from God, but as being of the very essence of what God is. When that happens, it will have an inevitable knock-on effect on our redeemed humanity and our view of love.

We must not forget the explosive impact that John's statement about God must have had on the ears of the original recipients of his letter. In the broad religious ethos of their day the idea of love associated to deity was not very prominent. Centuries, if not millennia, of pagan religion – even the refined versions of the Greek and Roman world – had a view of gods who were anything but loving. In reality, pagan theology was no more than a large-screen projection of humanity. The gods were the perceived supermen and superwomen of the religious mind. Great as they were, they still shared the foibles and failings of the human beings on whom they were modelled. Although they were to be worshipped and appeased, they were hardly to be admired or emulated.

Yet here is the apostle John saying, 'God is love'. What does he mean? Clearly, his choice of words is meant to point, not merely to what God does, but to what God *is* in his being. Only as this statement about God is put alongside the other jigsaw pieces of God's self-disclosure in the Bible do we realise that it is speaking of the mind-boggling uniqueness of the God of the Bible. Since God shows himself not merely to be one, but three-in-one, he is the God who has eternally existed in living, loving relationship. John expresses this truth with reference to Jesus, the eternal

Word of God, when he says, '...the Word was with (literally, *towards*) God...' (John 1.1). In other words, Jesus, the second Person of the Trinity, ever existed looking away from himself towards his fellow-Persons of the Godhead in an expression of eternal love. The same, of course, can be said of God the Father and God the Holy Spirit. Where there is God there is love, because where there is God there is relationship.

The self-denying profundity of this divine love can be glimpsed in the way that the relationships between Father, Son and Spirit are described. Of his relationship with the Father Jesus says that he loves to do his will (John 4.34; Matt. 26.39). Of the Holy Spirit, we hear God call him, 'My Spirit...' (Joel 2.28-29; Acts 2.17-18), an expression of intimacy of relationship, and we see him as the constant attendant of the incarnate Christ (see e.g., Matt. 3.16; 4.1; 12.28). There is nothing shallow about the love of God. It is both robust and passionate in the extreme.

The glory of this love is that it does not remain inaccessible within the confines of the transcendent God, but spills over into the experience of God's people, both in their relationship with him and their relationship with each other.

Recognising and receiving the love of God

John deliberately challenges the point of reference of love in his readers. Our fallen human nature has given us the misguided instinct to make self the centre of our own little universe. Thus, even in Christian experience, we are inclined to analyse our faith and salvation in terms of our

coming to an awareness of God and our moving towards him in faith and repentance. Thus in terms of the element of love in the relationship between God and his people the focus tends to give priority to the love of the individual.

John knocks this notion firmly on the head with his bold statement: 'In this is love, not that we loved God, but that He loved us and sent His Son to be the propitiation for our sins' (1 John 4.10). In one fell swoop he sets before us both the priority and the magnitude of God's love.

In terms of identifying the love of God as the initiating factor behind redemption, John is simply echoing the same truth which reverberates with increasing impact throughout the unfolding message of Scripture. The language he chooses to express this truth is among the warmest used in the Bible. The apostle Paul opts for a more theological and technical approach, but nevertheless encapsulates the same seed-truth. He talks frequently about foreknowledge, election and predestination, words which in the minds of many Christians have the coldest and most controversial connotations. Yet Paul uses them to convey the fact that the dimensions of the divine love stretch back beyond the limits of personal experience, even beyond the limits of time itself, into eternity past.

God's foreknowledge of his children (Rom. 8.29; 11.2; 1 Peter 1.2) has often been misconstrued as referring to God's ability to foresee events which are still future. Thus it is taken to mean that God responds to those who choose him in faith and in turn chooses them for inclusion in his family. Such a view rests more on the English word 'foreknow' and its related words than the Greek words and Hebrew concepts which underlie them. The latter

convey the sense of God setting his love on people in advance – loving them before they are born, or even before the world was created. The way in which the act of sexual union is translated in some versions as, for example, 'Adam *knew* Eve his wife and she conceived...' (Gen. 4.1), captures the sense of how love is involved in knowing someone. God's love predates all others.

Likewise, the doctrines of election and predestination have often been stripped of any sense of being expressions of love on God's part. Too often they have been propounded as the actions of a cold and clinical God, or else perceived in that way. Yet there again the Bible presents them wrapped up in the love of God, bringing these truths home in a way that could never be appreciated by mere logic. God's choice in election and his unsolicited love are used interchangeably in his description of Israel's spiritual roots (Deut. 7.6-11). His predestination is said to be an act of love designed to bring about the adoption of his people into his family (Eph. 1.4-5) and the conforming of their lives to the life of Jesus (Rom. 8.29).

John leaves us in no doubt that God's love stretches back before the beginning of time and was not in any sense a response to something he saw in us. God's children must recognise the initiative of a loving Father in bringing about their salvation and inclusion in the heavenly family.

The magnitude of God's love is evident in John's words about the lengths to which God went in order to secure the redemption of his people: '...and sent his Son to be the propitiation for our sins' (1 John 4.10). The word 'propitiation' may not mean much to the average reader of our day, but to those reading John's epistle for the first

time it was a word that was all too potent. It was the language of sacrifice, in particular the kind of sacrifice which was designed to turn aside the anger of the gods. Here John is saying (and he is only echoing what is stated elsewhere in the New Testament) that God sent his own Son, Jesus, to suffer that fate and to divert the divine wrath away from sinners.

It is the mystery of what took place on Mount Calvary when Jesus died on the cross. The psalmist, anticipating what would happen, spoke of a time when 'Mercy and truth have met together; Righteousness and peace have kissed' (Psalm 85.10), a time when all that seems irreconcilable in God's dealings with sinners is reconciled. Paul raises the same issue in a slightly different way when he speaks of God maintaining his integrity in being 'just and the justifier of the one who has faith in Jesus' (Rom. 3.26). How can God be consistent with himself as the just and holy One and yet welcome sinful people into his family? The cross provides the only answer which makes any sense, namely that Jesus took the place of his people in that momentous event, bore their sin and guilt, and as he died suffered the punishment of God's righteous anger which they deserved, thus simultaneously satisfying the demands of God's justice and opening the floodgates of God's love. Never was a father's love like this!

True Christian self-understanding must begin with at least some recognition of the extravagance of God's love and what it means to have received it through faith in Jesus Christ. The wonder of this new state, enjoyed through faith in Jesus Christ, is thrown into sharper relief by the contrast with what we once were. Jesus puts it bluntly in

an exchange with the Jews who refused to believe in him.
He says, 'You are of your father the devil' (John 8.44). He
is not being belligerent or provocative, but rather he is
stating an uncomfortable home-truth to a group of
religiously respectable people who were deluded about
their relationship with God.

The love of God is magnified when we realise the change
of father we have undergone in the move from being fallen
to being redeemed.

Responding to God's love

Going back to the first letter of John and his reflections
on the love of God as Father to his children, it is clear that
John sees the need, not just to recognise this love, but to
respond to it in an appropriate fashion. Having declared
its grandeur (1 John 3.1-2), he goes on to call for action
on the part of those who have been its objects. 'Everyone
who has this hope in Him purifies himself, just as He is
pure' (1 John 3.3).

There is a certain magnetic force in genuine love, one
which draws the loved towards the lover. We see it put
beautifully in the Song of Solomon – that great Old
Testament celebration of the love between a man and a
woman which also graphically illustrates the love between
Christ and his church. There we find a little phrase that
recurs three times, each time in a slightly altered state,
indicating how the love of the Beloved in the story blossoms
and comes of age.

We first hear it when the girl says, 'My beloved is
mine and I am his' (Song 2.16). Her love has a certain

self-centred orientation to begin with. But as the relationship develops, she comes to appreciate more of her suitor's love for her and it is not long before we hear the same words in a different form: 'I am my beloved's and my beloved is mine' (Song 6.3). She feels her own love to have paled somewhat alongside the love of this man who has set his affection upon her. Then finally we hear the words of a captivated woman: 'I am my beloved's' (Song 7.10). Her lover's love looms so large on her horizons that her own love for him is stripped of all self-interest and she gladly gives herself to him. This is the model for the church and her Lord. In the words of John the Baptist, 'He must increase, but I must decrease' (John 3.30).

There is no hint of bare asceticism in all of this. It is not as though there is any merit in self-denial, the notion that if it is painful, it must be good. Rather, it is the much repeated principle in Scripture that true gain in this fallen world can come only through loss. Seeking first God's kingdom, as opposed to ours (Matt. 6.33), being prepared to lose our lives to Christ in order that we should gain true life from him (Mark 8.35). This principle makes sense and leads to peace and fulfilment, when the focus is not upon self and sacrifice, but upon the Giver and what is gained.

In many ways it touches the very heart of our daily struggle as Christians. Charles Wesley knew something of it when he penned the words:

O Love divine, how sweet Thou art!
When shall I find my willing heart
All taken up with Thee?

I thirst, I faint, I die to prove
The greatness of redeeming love,
The Love of Christ to me.

The deepest longings of our hearts are drawn ever
upwards towards the God who has loved us to such a
degree, while we find ourselves sucked ever downwards
by the sinful instinct that refuses to relinquish the claim of
self to the throne of our lives. Even the great apostle Paul
agonised over this struggle in his lament on indwelling sin
(Rom. 7.13-25). Yet in the midst of the agony Paul's vision
of his beloved rescuer was never obliterated: 'O wretched
man that I am! Who will deliver me from this body of
death? I thank God – through Jesus Christ our Lord!'
(Rom. 7.24-25).

Although this divine love is attributed to Jesus in many
instances, it can never be divorced from the love of God
the Father. As his children respond to his Son, they respond
also to him. The love of God the Son will inevitably and
inexorably draw us deeper into the loving embrace of God
the Father.

Love which is a genuine response to God's love for us
will contain an element of fear. Not the servile fear that
cringes in the presence of power and authority, but what
is sometimes called filial fear – the appreciation mingled
with respect that is present in a child's relationship with
his or her father. Paul explains its meaning as he describes
to the Christians of Galatia what is involved in conversion.
It is the transition from slave to son (Gal. 4.7). A new
relationship with God leads to an altogether new perception
of God. No longer is he the God for whom people must
slave in order to win his favour (and ever be doomed to

fail in that quest), but is instead the great God who has loved sinners and provided all that is needed for their complete deliverance.

It does not in any sense rob God of his greatness, or attempt to bring him down to a merely human level. There have been some in recent years who have latched on to the '*Abba*, Father' God and ended up insulting him through a failure to afford him the respect he deserves. Paul demonstrates that there is no contradiction between showing God the highest reverence and respect because of who he is and what he is like, and enjoying the most intimate relationship with him as his precious children. Indeed, both elements of our response to God are closely intertwined and mutually enhance each other.

There is a well worn path which brings God's children in to the inner sanctum of his presence. His gift of the Holy Spirit as the 'Spirit of Adoption' actually enables us to claim our rights as children, purchased by Christ (John 1.11-12), and to enjoy the intimacy of fellowship with God, calling him, in the most endearing terms, '*Abba*, Father' (Rom. 8.15). But that privilege can be valued and cherished only when we remember that the God we address as 'Father' is the God who is also our Judge. He is the One who, as we have seen, has made full provision through his own Son for all that is needed to bring sinners into his family.

Being able to appreciate the glory of the God who is our Father will lead to a new appreciation of our exalted status as his children. Truly we are the children of a King.

Revelling in the love of God

There is such a thing as child-like pride and joy in a loving father. Many sons and daughters have glowed with satisfaction when their father has been honoured in some way. 'That's *my* Dad!', they think or say. There is pleasure for them in the honour that is his. They find pleasure in who he is and what he has done. They revel in their relationship.

John, the apostle, indulges in some sanctified revelling when he utters those words, 'Behold what manner of love the Father has bestowed upon us, that we should be called the children of God!' (1 John 3.1). This revelry basks in the stunning fact that the One who is our Father is none other than God himself: 'Now we are the children of *God*' (1 John 3.2). The broad spectrum of earthly paternity – a diversity of privilege which often divides people – is totally eclipsed for Christians by their divine paternity. Regardless of their social background, all Christians stand on the same footing by virtue of their relationship with God through Christ.

Thus, as our knowledge of God grows, our love for God deepens. As we have an increasing awareness of how great he is, we have a corresponding increase in our sense of privilege in calling him 'Our Father, who art in heaven ...'. We revel in who he is for his own sake.

Then as we look around us, through eyes which have been opened by his saving grace, the whole world takes on a different complexion and meaning. We are able to sing, in the words of Maltbie D. Babcock:

This is my Father's world,
And to my list'ning ears,
All nature sings, and round me rings
The music of the spheres.
This is my Father's world:
I rest me in the thought
Of rocks and trees, of skies and seas;
His hand the wonders wrought.

This is my Father's world,
The birds their carols raise,
The morning light, the lily white,
Declare their Maker's praise.
This is my Father's world:
He shines in all that's fair;
In the rustling grass I hear him pass,
He speaks to me everywhere.

This is my Father's world,
O let me ne'er forget
That though the wrong seems oft so strong,
God is the Ruler yet.
This is my Father's world:
The battle is not done;
Jesus who died shall be satisfied,
And earth and heav'n be one.

Every facet of the world and life is now coloured by God's involvement in it all, not merely as the sovereign Lord of all the universe, but as the wise and loving Father of his children. Indeed the force of this truth is dramatically pressed home when the apostle is able to say that absolutely everything which happens is under God's control and directed towards the ultimate good of each of his children (Rom. 8.28).

To be able to stop and reflect periodically on these truths has a transforming effect on our confidence and joy in the Christian life. We will be sustained in the knowledge that not only is our world cradled in the loving, everlasting arms of God, but our lives are too (Deut. 33.27) – a graphic picture of a strong, but gentle Father who carries his precious and vulnerable little ones.

Such depths of appreciation of God and what he has done for us through Jesus Christ his Son can be plumbed only through the grace of adoption. The sheer extravagance of God's love is seen in that he went far beyond providing for our need of life in regeneration and satisfying the requirements of his law in justification, or even the demands of his holiness in our sanctification. He went as far as is conceivably possible by making us his own children through adoption. Adoption brings the sinner into the most sublime relationship with the God he has so grievously offended.

4

Jesus My Brother

The gospel allows us to look at the Person and work of Christ from many different angles, each having something unique and vital to contribute to our understanding of salvation. There is one perspective which has often been overlooked and in some cases deliberately dismissed – he is Elder Brother to those who believe. As we see the basis of recognising Jesus in this capacity and begin to explore its ramifications, we are brought into a richer understanding of our redeemed relationship with God through him.

Our warrant for regarding Jesus in this way is found most explicitly in the book of Hebrews. There we read:

For both He who sanctifies and those who are being sanctified are all of one, for which reason He is not ashamed to call them brethren, saying: 'I will declare Your name to My brethren; In the midst of the assembly I will sing praise to You' (Heb. 2.11-12).

The family tie between Jesus and his people is signalled in two ways by this statement. In the first place there is the plain fact that he calls his people his brothers and his sisters. This not only picks up on the language of Psalm

22, from which the writer is quoting, but also alludes to
what Jesus himself said in this vein. His natural family
had come to press him to take a lower public profile and
the message was passed through the crowd to Jesus, 'Look,
Your mother and Your brothers are standing outside,
seeking to speak to You' (Matt. 12.47). Jesus' response,
which must have shocked the family among whom he had
grown up, was to point to his disciples and say, 'Here are
My mother and My brothers! For whoever does the will
of My Father in heaven is My brother and sister and
mother' (Matt. 12.49-50). From this early stage in his
ministry, Jesus was indicating a breadth to his family
relationships which went beyond that which met the eye.

The same truth is endorsed by the statement, 'both He
who sanctifies and those who are being sanctified are all
of one' (Heb. 2.11). The expression translated 'of one'
has reference to family associations and is reflected in the
different versions. It can either be taken as a reference to
having a common Father,[10] or else to belonging to the
same family.[11] The point is that the relationship between
Jesus and his people is so close that they can rightly be
said to belong to the same spiritual family, a family in
which he is a Brother. In order to establish the fact that
Jesus is not just any brother, but is the Elder Brother in
God's family, we must look elsewhere.

In his letter to the Romans, Paul alludes to the position
of Jesus within the divine family as he describes the
outworking and purpose of God's plan of redemption. The
goal of salvation is ultimately to glorify the Lord Jesus
Christ as he becomes 'the firstborn among many brethren'
(Rom. 8.29), that in the redeemed family of God Christ

might have the pre-eminence both as the Eternal Son of God and also as occupying the supreme place of honour among his brothers and sisters. The position of the firstborn in the family life of the ancient world had connotations, not merely of age, but also of rank and status, rights and responsibilities.

This truth about Jesus opens fresh windows on what he has done in bringing salvation and the nature of the salvation he has brought.

He identifies with his people

Right at the very centre of this truth lies the fact that Jesus had to be intimately identified with those he came to save. The passage from Hebrews cited above goes on to say: 'Therefore, in all things He had to be made like His brethren, that He might be a merciful and faithful High Priest in things pertaining to God, to make propitiation for the sins of the people' (Heb. 2.17). This is the language of necessity. If Jesus had not come in this capacity, he could not have fulfilled what was required for the salvation of his people. This has implications for what was taking place in the incarnation.

In order for Christ to save his people, he had first to be made like them in every way. The reason for this is bound up with God's covenant dealings with the human race. It was because of the federal relationship between Adam and the rest of humanity that the sin of which he was guilty had repercussions for the whole race descended from him. As Paul puts it, 'through one man sin entered the world, and death through sin, and thus death spread to all men,

because all sinned...' (Rom. 5.12). So for that damage to
be reversed, another federal head and representative had
to be provided; one who would perfectly correspond to
the needs of his people in order to deliver them from sin.
Thus Adam's relationship to the human race in a negative
sense is mirrored by what Jesus is to it positively. One
was the bringer of sin and death, the other of righteousness
and life.

The writer to the Hebrews develops this with particular
reference to the office and function of Christ as High Priest.
The essence of the priest's role was to represent others: to
go to God on their behalf and mediate for them. He had
to make sacrifice for their sins and intercede on their behalf
in prayer. He too had to be one of the people in order to
act as their representative. He had to be 'taken from among
men' (Heb. 5.1). He could not be an outsider, no matter
how impressive or worthy he might be. So Jesus, who is
the ultimate and perfect priest of his people, must have
this qualification.

If God's promised Saviour was to be the covenant head
of his new humanity, he had to be related to those he had
come to deliver. Hence when Jesus came into the world
as the Saviour of men, it was necessary for him to become
man. He had to take to himself 'a true body and a
reasonable soul'.[12] To save human beings, he had to
become human. His uniqueness was safeguarded in the
way he was conceived in the womb of Mary – a woman
who had never had sexual relations with any man – not
through human paternity, but by the power of the Holy
Spirit, thus allowing Jesus to take his humanity from his
mother without sharing the sin of her race.

This need for Jesus to be identified in the closest possible sense with his people lies at the heart of his insistence upon being baptised by his cousin John in the river Jordan (Matt. 3.13-17). John was understandably perplexed by Jesus' request, knowing full well that his was a baptism for the repentance of sins and Jesus had no apparent sins of which to repent! He protests quite rightly that their roles ought really to be reversed and he, 'the Baptist', instead ought to be baptised by Jesus (Matt. 3.14). But, in order to do all that was required for the salvation of sinners – 'to fulfil all righteousness' (Matt. 3.15) – he was baptised into identification with them, even in the very depths of their need.

As we reflect on the mystery of the incarnation – the coming together of humanity and deity in the Person of Jesus – we catch something of the glory of salvation itself. Jesus came to bring people back to a relationship in which they had fallen and from which they had been expelled: a living relationship with God. All of this hinged on their being joined to him by faith.

His intimacy with his people

We have already seen that in the whole process of creation, God was involved uniquely in the creation of man.[13] He engaged himself in this particular creative act in such a way that he was demonstrating a love for and fellowship with this one creature that was not true of his relationship with any other part of creation. God had, as it were, pressed his face into the face of Adam, imparting the ultimate kiss of life. From the outset in creation there was an intimate

bond between God and the human race. It should not surprise us, then, that in God's new creation the same should be true. When we look at how it comes about, we discover that this new intimacy transcends anything that existed by virtue of what God did in the beginning.

The origins of God's new creation are to be found in Jesus Christ. We are all familiar with Paul's statement about inclusion in this new order, 'Therefore, if anyone is in Christ; he is a new creation: old things have passed away; behold, all things have become new' (2 Cor. 5.17). This statement, at least as it appears in most English translations, is generally taken to refer to the believer's existential relationship with Christ and the consequences that flow from it. That element is certainly there, but on closer inspection it seems that Paul is saying something much more profound and even more glorifying to Jesus. If we were to render this statement more literally, it would simply read, 'Therefore, if anyone is in Christ: new creation!' The focus of the text actually changes from the believer and what he or she has become to Christ as the One who makes all things new. The person who is joined to Christ through new birth and saving faith does not merely undergo a radical change in all that he or she is as a private individual, but also becomes incorporated through Christ into something gloriously and infinitely new. Thus our horizons on salvation are raised to altogether higher levels than are often the norm in Christian circles today. Horizons which find their focus in Jesus with an overwhelming sense of awe and wonder. He is the epicentre of this new creation and in him alone it holds together (Col. 1.17) because he is the One who brought it into being.

To appreciate the mechanics of this, we must go back to the incarnation: the point at which divine plan becomes action. Here we find God being bound up with the human race, not merely by engaging with man in creative action, but by becoming man in an unprecedented and condescending initiative. The infinite and eternal Creator took upon himself the confines and limitations of his creature. Jesus became something which hitherto he had not been and in so doing established an intimacy between God and humanity which previously was inconceivable. In the Person of Jesus Christ, God was binding humanity to himself with unsurpassable intimacy; an intimacy which the human mind can only begin to appreciate and the human heart only attempt to feel when it is described in terms of family relations. The proverb, 'There is a friend who sticks closer than a brother' (Prov. 18.24), gives the inference that there is no closer bond we can enjoy in family life than that with a brother, yet in God's economy there is One who does come closer. He is a unique brother, God's one and only Son.

The intimacy between Christ and his people is prominent in his role as their Great High Priest. The High Priestly office of Christ is explored in detail in the book of Hebrews in which the readership being addressed find themselves under extreme duress in the faith, almost to the point of believing there is no-one who is able to understand or care. The writer is well aware of his own inadequacies and limitations in trying to come alongside these people under such circumstances, as so many pastors are in similar situations, so he directs them away from himself to someone greater. He highlights his unique

intimacy with those he represents by saying:

> We do not have a High Priest who cannot sympathise
> with our weaknesses, but was in all points tempted
> as we are, yet without sin (Heb. 4.15)

He is the perfect mediator because he has perfect
knowledge of the lives and circumstances of those on whose
behalf he is acting. Thus they are encouraged to come
with confidence through him to the God who is more than
able to help them in their time of need (Heb. 4.16).

This foundational gospel truth is designed to comfort
those who trust this Jesus and to reassure them that not
only is he interested in them uniquely, but also is involved
with them as no-one else ever could be as they go through
the struggles of this life. The very words that Jesus spoke
to his disciples prior to his departure were all intended to
reinforce the assurance that the intimacy they had known
with him while he was with them in bodily form would in
no way be lost or even diminished by his return to glory.
Repeatedly, both in the Upper Room and on the Mount of
the Ascension he says, 'I will not leave you...' (John 14.18;
Matt. 28.20). As there is a 'withness' within the Godhead
(John 1.1) which reflects intimacy of fellowship, so there
is the same between God and his people by virtue of their
relationship with Jesus, his Son – their Elder Brother.

His involvement with his people

When we begin to explore the way in which Jesus' intimacy
with his people is expressed, we see an involvement with

them which predates their own conscious awareness. The baffled Nathanael, shocked by the way Jesus seems to know him on their first encounter, asks, 'How do you know me? To which Jesus replies, '...when you were under the fig tree, I saw you' (John 1.48). Before a relationship is even established through salvation, an involvement exists.

Obviously this involvement is tied into God's purposes in election. It is the fact that it was 'in him [Christ]' that he chose his people from before the foundation of the world (Eph. 1.4). God's choice can never be separated from his Son and his chosen people can never understand themselves without tracing their spiritual roots to Christ, through Calvary back into the very depths of eternity.

It can also be argued that there is an eternal dimension to our understanding of justification.[14] The description of Jesus as 'the Lamb slain from the foundation of the world' (Rev. 13.8), takes us back to the roots of his justifying work, beyond Calvary into God's eternal decree. We are not permitted to forget the fact that Christ's involvement with his people begins before the beginning of time itself.

This eternal perspective on the way in which Jesus has been tied in with the lives of his people serves to safeguard for us the true proportions of our salvation in him. It is not as though his work on Calvary was not great in itself, but that the sum total is greater still, towering above time, space and history in the wise and loving purposes of the eternal triune God. It is only as our appreciation of the greatness of our salvation is stretched to its true limits, that our enjoyment of peace and assurance in that salvation is correspondingly stretched and strengthened in the face of everything which would undermine it.

Of course, we would be falling far short of a true grasp of Christ's involvement with his people if we confined ourselves to God's eternal plan of salvation. It is necessary to see how it is worked out in practice. It is in that sphere of space and time that the reality of this Elder Brother's love is both seen and felt in human experience. The parable of the prodigal son brings out certain crucial elements of this.

Although the popular title attributed to this parable makes its focus the wandering younger brother, there is a strong case for saying that the real focus of Jesus' teaching in this episode was really the elder brother and those he represents. Jesus' parables always had a punch line – a central thrust – and however interesting and helpful the other details in the story-line might be, they must never be allowed to obscure this central message. One of the best ways to discover a parable's centre of gravity is to look at the context in which it was spoken and the original audience at whom it was directed. When we turn up Luke's account of this dramatic tale, we find that it was occasioned by complaints from the religious leaders about Jesus' involvement with tax collectors and sinners and was specifically aimed at this self-righteous elite (Luke 15.1-3). The parable of the prodigal turns out to be the third in a series of stories in which the lost animal, object and person actually take second place to the one who goes to look for them.

The Jewish listeners, as they followed the details of the picture Jesus was painting, would have found their minds running ahead of him. In a sense they could see where Jesus was going. In their culture, with its understanding

of family responsibility, the crisis of a son who was lost was to some extent mitigated by an elder brother whose duty it was to go and find him. The twist in the tale lay, of course, in the fact that the elder brother did nothing of the sort and indeed was most indignant when his younger sibling turned up of his own accord and received such an enthusiastic welcome from their father (Luke 15.25-32).

This twist in the tale was designed to be the sting in the tail for the listening scribes and Pharisees. Jesus was reminding them of their duty to these erring fellow-countrymen in all their prodigality. They should have been like elder brothers to them. They ought to have gone searching for the spiritually lost in order to restore them to a lasting spiritual home. But they had failed.

The implication of Jesus' teaching at this point was that what the religious leaders had failed to be to the spiritually destitute, Jesus was. He was their true Elder Brother who would not rest until they were found.

We see this spelled out in terms of Jesus' understanding of his own mission in the incarnation: 'For the Son of Man has come to seek and to save that which was lost' (Luke 19.10). The global proportions of this statement are seen in the fact that Jesus did not physically accomplish this within the confines of his brief earthly ministry. In terms of the scale of this 'search and rescue mission', Jesus only scratched the surface during his brief and localised ministry. In his capacity as incarnate evangelist he was involved in the actual conversion of relatively few sinners. Yet the scope of his statement has reference to the purpose and consequence of his coming for the entire sweep of history and the total expanse of the globe. Indeed his

being 'firstborn over all creation' (Col. 1.15) and the fact
that even the inanimate world somehow longs for his return
(Rom. 8.19-23) show an intention to rescue, not just a
fallen race, but a fallen cosmos – something that was not
existentially accomplished during his time on earth.

The fulfilment of this grand statement must then be
found in the totality of Christ's coming and work, in
particular in its climax of his death, resurrection and
exaltation to glory. In that event-complex he once and for
all secured the redemption – in all its glorious dimensions
– which would then be applied through history until its
great consummation when Christ returns.

The once-and-for-all element of Jesus' searching and
saving mission cannot be divorced from its applicatory
element. The Christ who sought and saved is the One
who is actively involved in the on-going searching and
saving by his Spirit through his servants throughout the
world. This we shall consider in more detail when we
look at the ministry of the Holy Spirit in the family of
God.

The little glimpses we are allowed of Jesus' direct
involvement in this task while he was on earth show us
that his was a passionate involvement. He is ever the Christ
who is profoundly moved by the plight of the lost. Whether
it is as he moves around the towns and villages, seeing
multitudes and being 'moved with compassion for them,
because they were weary and scattered, like sheep having
no shepherd' (Matt. 9.36), or weeping over hard-hearted
Jerusalem (Matt. 23.37; Luke 13.34), we see a Saviour
who is truly concerned for those he has come to save.

There is a sense, I suppose, in which the saviours of

this world can be quite efficient and detached in the labours they pursue. Doctors, the emergency services and rescue workers can do a superb job and yet remain completely uninvolved with those whose lives they seek to preserve. In extreme cases the emotional impact of success and failure for some of these people can be little different. They are there to do a job and do it as professionally as possible – they can do no more. It can be hard for them to enter into the pain of loss.

But Jesus is not like that. It is not as though the perishing citizens of Jerusalem are beyond his power to save, but rather that they were not willing to be saved (Matt. 23.37). So we have this mysterious spectacle of the sovereign Son of God weeping over stubborn sinful rebels. We may not understand the mechanics of what is going on, but we cannot but feel the empathy of the Saviour.

The point is that the infinite and eternal God willingly and lovingly immerses himself in the task of rescuing people who have not given him a second thought. He is intimately involved with meeting human need.

The Brother who sets us free

In the ordinary experience of human family life, one of the joys of having an older brother – at least one who truly cares for you – is that he will introduce you to all the legitimate freedoms of family life. As the one who has the edge in terms of years and experience of growing up, he is the pioneer who has discovered the joys of life and is pleased to share them. (He will also, of course, be aware of life's dangers and pitfalls and will do his best to steer you away from them.) His relationship with his brothers

and sisters will have a truly liberating effect upon them. The reality of this is only found ideally and ultimately in relationship with Jesus as our perfect Elder Brother.

During a conversation with some Jews who had professed to believe in him Jesus speaks about this new freedom which is found through him (John 8.31-36). It developed into a somewhat heated exchange as to what constituted a true and liberating religion.

The Jews were balking at Jesus' assertion that in their natural state they were not free, but slaves (John 8.33), but Jesus presses home his point by saying, 'whoever commits sin is a slave to sin' (John 8.34), and showing them that they show more family resemblance to those whose father is the devil than those who truly belong to God (John 8.44). The acid test of fatherhood is the question of whose voice they will listen to. Their refusal to recognise or receive his words, which were the words of God, is the proof that they have not received life from God (John 8.37, 43). Thus, despite their outward veneer of religion and apparently commendable interest in Jesus, the fundamental problem of their lives still remained: they were under the domination of sin and could not break free. Jesus holds out to them the offer of liberty.

The way he expresses it is interesting. First of all he says, 'You shall know the truth and the truth shall make you free' (John 8.32). Then he puts a finer point on it by saying, 'If the Son makes you free, you shall be free indeed' (John 8.36). What they perceived to be freedom within the confines of a distorted Jewish religion was nothing more than an illusion that could be replaced with reality only if they came to Christ.

By expressing it this way, John is giving a major clue as to how a person comes to enjoy this liberating union and communion with Jesus in a meaningful way. At the beginning of his Gospel, he introduces Jesus as the eternal 'Word' (John 1.1) – the Greek expression is *Logos* – thus fixing in his readers' minds the link between the everlasting absolute God and everlasting absolute truth. In so doing, he cleverly straddles the cultural divide of his day between Jews and Greeks. The former had their thoughts on the eternity of personified Wisdom (see, for example, Prov. 3.19-20); the thinking of the latter was dominated by the various strands of philosophical thought, and they were aware of the concept of self-existent and absolute truth. Hence John was priming the minds of his readers to see the link between Jesus and truth. Later on in his Gospel we find John exclusively reporting the words of Jesus when he said, 'I am the way, *the truth* and the life...' (John 14.6). Translate these details into the means by which we actually engage with Jesus and he with us and we see that it is through his living Word – the Bible. Through Scripture he addresses himself to the mind and through the mind to the heart, drawing out a response of faith and obedience. Our experience of Jesus can never be divorced from our knowledge of his Word.

Paul deals with the implications of this at much greater length in his letter to the Galatians, a group of Christians who were being influenced by Judaisers – those who wanted to make obedience to the Mosaic Law a requirement for salvation. He points out to these believers that they are simply tying themselves in knots with a new list of rules and regulations which have robbed them of

the freedom they had started to enjoy through the gospel of grace which Paul had preached to them.

It is not only those who live lives of blatant wickedness who are slaves to sin; even those for whom religion has become a god and an end in itself, are not free in the way that they long to be.

Jesus presents himself as the antidote. As the truth of his word lays hold on the minds and hearts of those who hear, it begins to expose their own way of life for what it is and then goes on to point to what it could be through faith in Jesus Christ. The truth of God, then, is not some bare abstraction, but Someone rich and personal, none other than the Son of God himself. To know him, that is, to be brought into saving union with him, is to have eternal life (John 17.3) and so to experience the abundant life that Jesus promises to his children (John 10.10).

He is the true antidote for sin. It was Martin Luther who described sin as having left man *incurvatus in se* – turned in upon himself. Man's whole life-orientation has become the polar opposite to what God intended it to be. But Christ the Son restores life's true God-centred polarity – the only way in which we can be released to enjoy the full potential of humanity.

The brotherliness of Jesus, then, emanates from eternity past, is manifest in space and time through his coming into the world as seeker of the lost and spiritually homeless to do all that is needed for their recovery, then spills over into the sweep of human history as the One who builds God's family. The final frame in this sequence, so to speak, is the Brother who shares in the joy of the Father who presides over his reunited family (contrast the resentment

of the elder brother of the parable [Luke 15.28]) and who
eternally is the living link between these children and their
God.

5

His Spirit and Mine

We have considered the implications of the new relationship we enjoy with God through salvation in terms of relationship with God the Father and with God the Son. Human logic, as much as divine revelation in Scripture, would raise our expectation that there must also be a strand of this relationship which brings us into fellowship with the third Person of the Trinity: God the Holy Spirit. We do not have to look far to discover that this is indeed the case. It becomes clear that he is the One who actually and personally earths the reality of this planned and provided salvation in the lives of those who are God's children.

It is sad in many ways that the rediscovery of the Holy Spirit which has swept through the churches of the world in the twentieth century has in many ways missed the point of who he is and what he does. The very mention of his name in many evangelical circles today evokes the reflex word associations of 'signs and wonders', 'tongues and prophecy', or the like. The Spirit theology which has become the accepted norm for many, rather than giving honour to the Holy Spirit, has ironically verged on becoming an insult to him by almost completely overlooking his quiet, but vital work in the conversion and nurture of the children of God. The fact that the

Corinthian epistles form the major quarry from which a contemporary understanding of the Spirit is hewn and the fact that the Corinthian Church was actually being rebuked for its immature theology and behaviour do not seem to connect in the minds of many evangelical readers!

To say that the Person of the Holy Spirit was not paraded in high profile by the theologies of a former generation may well be true. However, this does not mean that his presence and work did not pervade those theologies in a manner which actually reflects the way he is presented in Scripture itself. He is, as has often been noted, the self-effacing member of the Trinity.

If it is not demeaning to make the comparison, it is frequently true to say that those who are quiet by nature are full of surprises when others probe beneath the veil of superficial appearances. Thus the Holy Spirit who tends to have a 'behind the scenes' role in much of the outworking of God's redemption is actually more prominent and crucial in the experience of that salvation than is usually acknowledged. To be able to say as a Christian that God's Spirit is my Spirit is a truly remarkable privilege.

The tripartite relationship

Those who are unfamiliar with the technical language that theologians are wont to use are to be forgiven if the doctrine of 'the double procession' of the Holy Spirit conjures up images of carnival parades! (Theological terms are in constant need of translation into the common language of every generation.) The term expresses an important truth,

but one which needs to be unpacked before it can be appreciated to the full.

The term 'double procession' is intended to express the way in which the three Persons of the Godhead co-exist and work together both with regard to their relationship with each other and their relationship with the world and universe. Thus, in the language of the Nicene Creed, the Holy Spirit is said to 'proceed from the Father and the Son'. This simply encapsulates in one line what Jesus expressed in a development of thought in the Upper Room discourse. There, on the eve of his departure from the disciples and eventual return to glory, he not only promises that the Father will send the Holy Spirit to them (John 14.16, 26), but that he too would be involved in sending the Heavenly Paraclete for their comfort and support (John 16.7). When he tells them that the Holy Spirit will be '*another* Helper' (John 14.16), he uses the Greek word *allon*, which means in essence, 'another of the same kind'. Thus he was assuring them of continuity in the relationship with God they had begun to enjoy in and through him. Indeed they were soon to discover that there would be more than mere continuity: the Holy Spirit would take them into glorious new realms of intimate fellowship with God which previously were unimaginable.

As the disciples were being introduced to God the Holy Spirit, they were also being prepared to see and appreciate him in his presence and role within the family of God. He himself would lead them into these truths as the message of the New Testament was to unfold through their ministries.

It was as though two great areas of truth were being set

before them in parallel. On the one hand their understanding of God was being broadened to appreciate that
'Hear, O Israel: The LORD our God, the LORD is one'
(Deut. 6.4) actually involved a three-ness as well as oneness. Although there were references hinting at plurality
within the Godhead in the Old Testament, it was only
with God's fuller revelation of himself in the New that he
is seen to be the great Three in One. As they explored
these new-found truths, so they became increasingly aware
of the amazing inter-relationships within the Godhead.
On the other hand they were learning that the Holy Spirit
was involved in establishing, sustaining and guaranteeing
their relationship with God in a breath-taking fashion.

The combined effect of this was to elevate their
appreciation of knowing God to new heights. So much so
that Peter could refer to the privileges of the Christian life
in terms of being made 'partakers of the divine nature' (2
Peter 1.4) – a level of intimacy with God which no Old
Testament saint was in a position to grasp fully. There are
a number of ways in which the Spirit's involvement with
the children of God profoundly affects their enjoyment of
the blessings of his family.

The animator of the soul

One of the most dramatic insights we are given into the
Spirit's work in conversion is when the apostle Paul brings
us, as it were, into the spiritual labour ward in the book of
Romans. As the struggles of a mother in labour and the
tension of a father in waiting are rewarded by that first cry

that goes up from their new-born child – the first manifest sign that there is life, so the first indicator of new life in the believer is the cry of the soul that goes up to God. The first clear evidence of the Spirit's presence in the life of the believer is the fact that he or she cries out, '*Abba, Father*' (Rom. 8.15). This statement deserves reflection as it touches upon our experience of the Christian life at a number of points.

Clearly it takes us right back to the moment this new life began and the evidence that it was really there. From the very outset, the Spirit is involved as the One who imparts that life. In our natural state as human beings, we are 'dead in trespasses and sins' (Eph. 2.1). We are spiritually inert, devoid of that vital relationship with God which animates the soul. The implications of that are enormous. We see it in the encounter between Jesus and Nicodemus in which this exceptionally religious man was told that unless he was born again he would continue to be both blind to and unaffected by the spiritual realities of the Kingdom of God (John 3.3,5). Jesus defines this new birth in terms of being 'born from above' (John 3.3) – the Greek word translated 'again' can also bear the meaning 'from above' – and being 'born of the Spirit' (John 3.5-6). The obvious play on words in the first case paves the way for the reference to the Spirit's involvement in the second case.

The point is that the moment when new life begins, spiritually speaking, is the moment when the Holy Spirit works in regenerating power in the life of an individual. From that point onwards their consciousness of God takes on new dimensions. For the first time they see him, not

only as the One who will judge, but also as the One who will save through his Son. The first conscious expression of this new life is the cry of repentance and faith which turns them away from the world and from themselves, towards God and his mercy and grace in Jesus Christ. This motif of new birth from the Spirit of God as the starting point of Christian experience is John's favourite way of describing the existential origins of Christian life.

Paul uses different imagery to describe the same truth. We have already made reference to Paul's use of 'new creation' (2 Cor. 5.17) to portray the dramatic new beginning a convert undergoes. This inevitably mirrors the Spirit's involvement in the origin of the natural world and universe as the One who 'was hovering over the face of the waters' (Gen. 1.2). Out of the void of spiritual death, the Spirit brings the glory of spiritual life.

A more frequently used metaphor in Paul's writings on this subject is that of resurrection. As it is put in Romans, there is a 'newness of life' which comes from being raised up together with Christ 'through the glory of the Father' (Rom. 6.4).[15] The description of the resurrection of Jesus as being accomplished by 'the Glory of the Father' would seem to refer to the outpouring of his power in that event[16] – an allusion to the Spirit's involvement. The same truth is expressed in the letter to the Ephesians when he says that those who were once spiritually dead are 'made alive together with Christ ... and raised up together' (Eph. 2.4-5).

In other words, the Holy Spirit's involvement in the Christian's beginnings is that of imparting life to the dead. He is the animator of the soul.

It is perhaps even more wonderful to realise that, great as the Spirit's re-creative work in regeneration is, it is enhanced marvellously by his continued involvement with God's new creatures. Again, if we go back to the genesis of all things, we see that God did not create and then retreat. Rather he made all things, then continued as the One who was closely involved with his world and universe as its upholder and provider. So the Spirit who initiates new life is the same Spirit who sustains that life through his indwelling the lives of God's children. He literally takes up residence within them as living temples of the Almighty (1 Cor. 6.19).

He is present in us and with us as the divine enabler of God's children. He is the One who puts the being into their life. Which brings us back to the cry of 'Abba, Father'.

Life and action

The life which the Spirit imparts translates into the action the Spirit enables. Paul's description of him as 'the Spirit of adoption' (Rom. 8.15) indicates that he empowers us for life and action which is orientated towards the family of God.

In the context of this passage in Romans the immediate focus of this action is found in the prayer life of the child of God. The Spirit of Adoption enables the believer's cry to reach out to God in his capacity as Father. Although it is true to say that people who are not Christians do pray, prayer outside a living relationship with God amounts to no more than 'vain repetitions' (Matt. 6.7) – there is a

dismal futility about such supposed communication with God because there is no true interaction involved. Even though the lofty words, 'Our Father who art in heaven...' may have been employed, there is no real sense in which God is known as Father with all that is invested in such closeness with him.

Only when the Spirit has worked and is present in the life of an individual can those precious words be spoken with authenticity.

As we have seen already the first true cry of 'Father' to God as Father comes in regeneration and conversion. It is the dawning of gospel truth which allows us to see that we no longer have to run from God as Judge, but can freely run to him as Saviour – the provider of life through his Son. If we go back to the labour ward for a moment, we are constantly being told of the importance of the bonding which takes place between new-born child and parents, even at the earliest stages of life. Even the unintelligible cry from the child which pierces the ward seems to be directed towards its parents and certainly strikes a chord in their hearts in a way it cannot with those who are merely the staff involved with the birth. There is, understandably, an aura of mystery about such a process which delves into our complexity as human beings. It ought not to surprise us to find a parallel element of mystery in the spiritual bonding which takes place between a new convert and God.

It can be hard to understand because pre-conversion we are by nature hostile to God (Rom. 8.7) – we are antagonised by who he is and what he requires. This hostility spills over into our attitude to his day, his house

and his people. Yet when new birth takes place, our heart is drawn out after him in love, faith and obedience. The simple cry of faith in conversion, 'God, save me!', is not of mere human origin, but evidence of the Spirit's having worked.

In our natural families, it is normal to expect the bonding process between children and parents to continue through childhood, the often stormy years of adolescence, right through to adulthood. The key to seeing that bond established is through developing communication. Put simply, relationships grow as those involved relate. At every point of this development in family experience, each step of progress is simply further proof of the blood ties which hold that unit together.

In the developing relationships between God and his children – they must always be developing, or else they stagnate – the measure of progress is also seen in the level of communication. It is not just our learning to listen to God, with the understood trust and obedience which is essential to hearing what he says, but also our learning to speak with him. I remember being quite intrigued when once I asked a well-known Christian preacher what the hardest part of the Christian life was for him after all these years. His response was, 'Sustaining a meaningful prayer life.' He knew, as so many of us know only too well, that it is possible to think we are speaking to God without actually communicating with him. Words are crossing our lips without really expressing either the real thoughts of our hearts or any genuine longing for God to understand and act.

So in Romans 8:15 when Paul talks about the Spirit's

involvement in this heart-cry to the Father, he is touching upon the marks of meaningful communion, not only at the birth-stage of the Christian life, but also at each sequential stage of development. Indeed the wider issues of Romans 8, many of which relate to the struggles of Christian experience and the need to persevere through them, drive home the necessity of the aid of the Spirit in prayer if we are to survive at all. Spiritual life in the believer is sustained through the Spirit's presence, a presence which is tangibly expressed through prayer.

The comfort of this truth of divine strength manifest in human weakness is seen in the moments of profound spiritual incapacity which even the best of God's children have from time to time. On those occasions, Paul tells us, 'the Spirit himself makes intercession for us with groanings which cannot be uttered' (Rom. 8.26). The thought which seems to be on the apostle's mind here is that when our words run out, the Spirit's words take over. There appears to be a link back to a few verses earlier to the comment about the believer groaning with the grinding pressure of living as a child of God in a fallen world (Rom. 8.23). Such is the bond between the Spirit of God and the child of God that the former can express the longings of the latter accurately, earnestly and effectively.

The Spirit of Adoption, then, plays a vital role in fostering meaningful communication through prayer within God's family.

The Spirit's Comfort

Paul also links the presence and ministry of the Spirit in the Christian's life to his or her assurance of faith and salvation. Immediately after his allusion to the Spirit of Adoption and his agency in prayer, he says, 'The Spirit himself bears witness with our spirit that we are the children of God' (Rom. 8.16). In the extremities of faith, the Spirit fulfils his promised role as Comforter.[17]

Often, the effect of trial, tribulation and persecution can be to create devastating doubt and uncertainty. This was evident in the experience of the Christians addressed in the book of Hebrews. The cost of commitment for at least some of them had become so great that they were on the verge of no longer regarding themselves as Christians and were instead reverting to Judaism. The Spirit's work, not only under such duress, but indeed in the ordinary course of things, is to confirm our sense of belonging to God along with our conviction that God will not let us go.

Some have regarded this 'inner witness' of the Spirit in a purely mystical sense, a kind of inner feeling of security. It is undoubtedly true that there is an element of this in the way God's Spirit works with us, but the very language that Paul uses would suggest there is more to it.

Paul's choice of words suggests something more substantial than merely the swaying of emotions and feelings; namely the presentation of evidence. He does this by pointing believers away from themselves in morbid introspection, to look away instead to Jesus Christ and God's full provision of salvation through him. Thus he goes on in this eighth chapter of Romans to martial the

evidence of what Christ has done for his children to guarantee the security of all who simply embrace him by faith. It is the fact that head and heart are inextricably linked in God's dealings with us that means there is more than mere intellectual persuasion involved in this witness-bearing.

There is, however, at least one instance where there is the promise that the Spirit will jump to the defence of God's children in an unusual way, and that is when they themselves are called to bear testimony for their Saviour. As Jesus sends out his disciples, first of all on a localised evangelistic mission, then on a wider mission which will take them to the Gentiles, he warns them of times when they will be hauled before courts for his sake. He comforts them in the face of this disturbing prediction by saying:

'But when they deliver you up, do not worry about how or what you should speak. For it will be given you in that hour what you should speak; for it is not you who speak, but the Spirit of your Father who speaks in you' (Matt. 10.19-20).

The comfort-value of this statement is immense, because of the allusion to the Father's involvement with the Spirit. The imagery is potent, since not a few minors have found themselves facing the dock in fear and trembling, but have been sustained as their father has stood with them and even spoken for them. So our Father in Heaven will, through his Spirit, stand with and speak for his children, even under hostile cross-examination.

The broad scope of this section in Matthew would tend

to argue against those who have tried to restrict this role of the Spirit just to the apostolic band under the New Testament dispensation. It is only reasonable to see the application of these words to all believers in every period of history, but perhaps even arguable to apply it to the testimony we are called upon to give in settings which are outside a formal court of law. There are certainly many Christians who can speak of occasions when they have been 'put on the spot', so to speak, about their faith and salvation and have found to their own amazement that words, train of thought and courage, complete with appropriate Bible references have sprung to mind and brought glory to their Saviour.

Filial Spirit

Putting together all these various dimensions of the Holy Spirit's work in the believer, we see him as the One who imparts and cultivates a filial spirit towards God that was not there by nature in fallen human beings and to which they have no natural right.

As it is by nature that we are 'children of disobedience' and 'children of wrath' (Eph. 2.2-3), so it is only through the new nature imparted by God's Spirit in regeneration and the gracious act of adoption which ensues through faith and repentance that we become the children of the living God. The Spirit's work is not only to bring about this new standing and relationship before God as he applies the finished work of Christ to those who believe, but also to foster in them a new self-understanding.

There is a right sense in which we should talk about

the renewed self-image of the believer. This does not come about through the power of positive thinking, or through less than honest self-appraisal, but rather through being helped to understand what we have now become and are entitled to by virtue of our union with Christ. In this way the filial element of the Holy Spirit's operation within God's family is worked out practically in sanctification.

The thrust of this, particularly in the New Testament letters, might be summed up in the exhortation, 'Be what you are!' The apostolic line of reasoning in these epistles, certainly as far as Paul is concerned, is to spend time expounding the reality of what has been accomplished by Christ and imparted to all who receive him by faith, and then call for personal response in light of that.

In one way it might be compared to a vagrant who has been rescued from a life on the street and given a home in a comfortable house, with a loving family. His former way of life and circumstances are so ingrained in him that the 'too good to be true' element of his new situation actually inhibits his full enjoyment of it. So it becomes necessary for someone from his new-found family to take him by the hand and show him, perhaps over and over again, the scope of his new life and entitlements.

So the Holy Spirit spends literally the lifetime of God's children doing this guided tour of what they have become in Christ and encouraging and enabling them to enter into the fullness of it in their day-to-day experience.

6

Pitied, Protected, Provided for and Chastened

We have spent time considering the relational element of this new life in the family of God, exploring the marvellous way in which each Person of the Godhead is closely involved with those who are redeemed. I now want to broaden our considerations to look at the actual benefits we receive in the context of these relationships, within the confines of the divine family.

The Westminster Confession of Faith expresses these benefits succinctly by saying, among other things, that those who are made partakers of the grace of adoption are 'pitied, protected, provided for and chastened by him as by a father'.[18] These practical blessings and privileges enumerated in the Confession are prefaced by one important detail, namely that every believer has the right of access to God as Father, indeed 'access to the throne of grace with boldness'.[19] The sheer privilege of prayer is something we should never treat lightly or dare to take for granted. It is quite true, as we have seen already, that the God we approach is an enthroned God. He has position, character and authority which would naturally preclude us as fallen beings from coming to him, or being able to

remain in his presence. Yet we are encouraged, in and through the Lord Jesus Christ, to come 'boldly' and with 'full assurance of faith' before God's throne that we might there claim for ourselves the benefits he bestows through his Son (Heb. 4.16; 10.22).

Sadly the impression of God's Fatherhood which dominates much Christian thinking has been coloured by the Victorian perception of what fathers were like; a distortion of what ought to be both normal and true. In many homes in that era, the father was seen as remote and austere by his children. Despite his acknowledged benevolence, he was not seen in any real sense as being approachable. The same attitude was present in parts of the United States where it was the norm for children to address their father as 'Sir'.

We are indeed expected to be reverent in our approach to God and appreciation of what he is like, but, amazingly, we are told that in no way ought this create inhibitions in our relationship with him. Reverence and intimacy are not mutually exclusive. The picture that is being painted in the book of Hebrews to Christians who had every reason to be afraid of God, because of their doubts and disobedience, is that of a child who has the confidence to run into the arms of his father and be sure of a loving reception.

The particular blessings of the Christian life can be experienced and enjoyed only when we have grasped the fact that we have a right of access to God by virtue of our relationship with his Son, Jesus. In his loving kindness and mercy he has provided all that is necessary to allow us to come to him and allow him to lavish the gifts of his

love upon us. This fact in a real sense puts a shine on all the privileges we receive as his children, because we know that they are given to us, not under duress, or because they have been extracted from him as a reluctant giver, but because he truly loves his children. We do not need to employ the services of Mary, saints or angels to twist God's arm into hearing and answering prayer. Nor do we need to think of Jesus as the Son who must cajole his Father into looking with compassion upon his church. Rather we see such perfect harmony within the Godhead that there is perfect unified love poured out by Father, Son and Holy Spirit which we are invited to enjoy.

What, then, are we to make of the specific benefits of life in God's family which we are entitled to appropriate and enjoy?

A God who understands

The complaint of many teenagers as they struggle with their fathers these days is 'Dad doesn't understand'. There is a generation gap, times have changed, he belongs to a different world.

Strangely, it is easy to feel that way about God. He certainly belongs to a different world, in that we are born into a Kingdom of Darkness while he is Lord of the Kingdom of Light: two realms that have nothing in common and have as much chance of mixing as oil and water. God responds to the silent complaint of his people through Isaiah by saying, 'Why do you say, O Jacob, and speak, O Israel: "My way is hidden from the LORD, and my just claim is passed over by my God"?' (Isa. 40.27).

They really thought he didn't understand.

It can often be our experience, especially when we find ourselves under the relentless pressures of life, that we feel as though there is no-one who can empathise or understand: no-one who truly cares. We have already considered the empathy that we find in the Person of Jesus Christ as our great High Priest,[20] God wants us to know that this is an empathy found in each Person of the Trinity, not least in God the Father.

Probably the most precious expression of the Father's understanding love and care is to be found in the book of Psalms.

> As a father pities his children, so the LORD pities those who fear him. For he knows our frame; he remembers that we are dust (Psalm 103.13-14).

There is a divine compassion which transcends the most profound compassion a child can know. A compassion which stirs the utmost confidence in God.

Following the human analogy which God employs here, we know that though there may be many aspects of a father's dealings with his children which they do not immediately understand or appreciate, if they are confident that he loves them and cares for them, they will trust him and go along with what he says. They will obey what he commands, they will accept his restrictions, they will follow his guidance. Their response to him is undergirded by the conviction that he knows them, knows what is best for them and will not do anything against their best interests.

So it is with the One who is our heavenly Father. There will be numerous occasions in his dealings with us as his children when we are left scratching our heads as to why he has allowed things to turn out in the way that they have. There are, as we sometimes say, 'unusual providences' which overtake us in the path of life. We will be able to accept such things only if we can have genuine confidence in the Lord who is behind them. This is particularly true of events and circumstances in life which are manifestly beyond all human control: the onset of illness, the birth of a handicapped child, sudden bereavement, or whatever. Those who find themselves in such situations instinctively want to cry out, 'Why this and why me, O Lord?' When we catch a glimpse of the compassion of the God in whose hands our lives are placed, it alleviates the pain and uncertainty, at least to some extent.

God assures us that he knows the kind of creatures we are. He knows us because he made us. He is fully aware of our limitations and capacities as finite human beings, not merely in a generic sense, but in a uniquely personal way. The Psalmist is elsewhere able to testify to God's amazing knowledge of him as a unique individual (Psalm 139.13-16). In the New Testament, Paul is able to assure the Corinthians that God will not allow any of them to be tempted or tried beyond the limits of what they could bear, indeed, he will always ensure that there is a way of escape for every situation (1 Cor. 10.13). The greatness of God does not leave him aloof from the fact that we his creatures are but dust, our bodies mere 'earthenware vessels' (2 Cor. 4.7). In loving condescension he accommodates himself to our level. As a natural father

will get down on his hands and knees to his little child crawling on the carpet, so our God and Father kneels down with us. He enters our little world.

The implications of this are worked out in detail. God knows the brevity of life, the mountains and valleys of human experience and the inevitability and aftermath of death (Psalm 103.15-16). Shakespeare's 'Seven Ages of Man' are predated by God's knowledge of the sweep of human experience – the many and varied 'changing scenes of life'. No matter where we might find ourselves on the spectrum of life, God knows what it is like for us. Right down to old age, the so-called twilight years of life, God knows circumstances, changes, feelings – absolutely everything associated with every stage of life's journey.

Such knowledge should be a source of enormous comfort and encouragement. If the evident empathy of a consultant or surgeon will help us to place our life in his hands, how much more our knowledge of this great Physician and his knowledge of us. There was a time in our own experience as a family when we were looking for help for our little daughter who is mentally handicapped. We had been round various professionals and specialists and were not entirely convinced that any of them could offer the kind of help we felt was needed. That was until we came across the staff of a specialist centre in Philadelphia. We listened to a series of lectures for several days which outlined the theory which lay behind their treatment and we had the overwhelming sense that for the first time we had found some people who really understood our daughter's needs and so felt confident in following the course of therapy they were recommending.

We have every warrant as Christians to entrust every detail of our lives to our God, not just because of who he is, but also because of how much he cares. The hymn-writer, William Freeman Lloyd, picks up a line from Psalm 31.15 encapsulating this truth and weaves it through a hymn of confidence in God:

My times are in Thy hand:
My God, I wish them there;
My life, my friends, my soul I leave
Entirely in Thy care.

My times are in Thy hand,
Whatever they may be,
Pleasing or painful, dark or bright,
As best may seem to Thee.

My times are in Thy hand:
Why should I doubt or fear?
A Father's hand will never cause
His child a needless tear.

My times are in Thy hand,
Jesus, the Crucified;
Those hands my cruel sins had pierced
Are now my guard and guide.

My times are in Thy hand:
I'll always trust in Thee;
And, after death, at Thy right hand
I shall forever be.

Truly we can trust the God who both knows us and cares for us.

My Faithful Protector

National security was always a big thing for God's people in Old Testament times. There was rarely a period in their history when they were not surrounded and outnumbered by hostile neighbours. Yet they were always assured of the protection of their covenant God. Indeed the fact that God chose to relate to them within the framework of covenant (Gen. 9.8-17; 15.9-21; 17.1-27; Exod. 19.1-24.18; 2 Sam. 7.5-16; Jer. 31.31-34) was something they were able to identify with in a very graphic way. The structure within which God's revelation unfolds is a general structure that was part of everyday life for all people of the ancient Mediterranean world.[21]

It was common practice in those days, under the terms of international law, for larger, more powerful kings to enter into relationships through treaties with smaller, less powerful kings. These suzerainty treaties, as they are often called, involved the pledge of protection from suzerain (the more powerful ruler) to vassal (the smaller state). This reassurance carries over into God's being legally bound to his people. He promises, indeed guarantees, to provide protection for them.

We see this aspect of God's character displayed in his being 'the Divine Warrior' – the mighty God who fights on behalf of his people.[22] He is the One who goes out to fight both with and for his people and their armies. Some of the most graphic examples of this are found in the books of Samuel and Kings.

On one occasion we see the Lord's intervention when David goes to attack the Philistines in the Valley of

Rephaim. God tells him, 'When you hear the sound of marching in the tops of the mulberry trees then you shall advance quickly. For the LORD will go out before you to strike the camp of the Philistines' (2 Sam. 5.24). When he obeyed God's instructions, victory came as promised.

On another occasion when the prophet Elisha was being pursued by the army of the Syrians and had been surrounded at Dothan, his servant panicked at the sight of this huge force which had hemmed them in. The response of his master was to say, 'Do not fear, for those who are with us are more than those who are with them' (2 Kings 6.16). He goes on to pray that the servant's eyes might be opened by God. When this happened he saw that the mountains around the town were full of horses and chariots of fire – a battalion of heavenly protectors (2 Kings 6.17). God then proceeds to strike the Syrians with blindness so that his children are kept safe.

Many other instances could be cited: God's deliverances during the Exodus and conquest of the land of Canaan; the confrontation between David and Goliath when the young fighter says, 'I come to you in the name of the LORD of hosts whom you have defied' (1 Sam. 17.45); and others besides.

The point is, as we find stated in the Proverbs, 'In the fear of the LORD there is strong confidence. And his children will have a place of refuge' (Prov. 14.26). His protection is not merely afforded as King to his subjects, but as Father to his children. Indeed the ferocity of that protection can be seen when God says of his children, 'He who touches you touches the apple of My eye' (Zech. 2.8). 'The apple of the eye' was a Hebrew idiom for the

pupil of the eye. God was referring to the reflex protective action that a person makes when someone else comes anywhere near touching that most sensitive part of the body. Such is the speed and effectiveness of his protective care of his children.

Nor is this truth confined to the Old Testament. The Father we address in the Lord's Prayer is the One we appeal to for deliverance from evil (Matt. 6.13). He always has been and always will be the protector God.

All I have needed, Your hand has provided

The psalmist was able to testify concerning God from of old, 'No good thing will he withhold from those who walk uprightly' (Psalm 84.11). It is in the very heart of God to provide his children with everything that will be good for them. God had proved this to his people in his dealings with them through successive generations – despite their complete unworthiness.

When he led them out of slavery in Egypt to a new land and a new beginning, it is no second rate real estate he passes on to them, but a 'land flowing with milk and honey' (Exod. 3.8) – a fact confirmed by the twelve spies when they returned from their first reconnaissance mission to Canaan carrying the most sumptuous fruit (Num. 13.23). Yet somehow his people managed to persist in questioning both his desire and ability to provide.

Jesus puts the issue beyond question in the Sermon on the Mount when he challenges those who are forever worrying about how they will get what they need for life. (The truth is that it is more often than not the luxuries of

life as opposed to its necessities that they are anxious to acquire.) Jesus points to the most insignificant components of creation: sparrows, blades of grass, meadow flowers and troublesome ravens. They are worthless in the eyes of men, yet their needs are more than adequately met by the God who is *'your* Father' (Matt. 6.26). Once more the sheer loveliness of what God is like, has done and continues to do for his people is captured in the lyrics of the popular hymn by Thomas O. Chisholm:

'Great is Thy faithfulness', O God my Father,
There is no shadow of turning with Thee;
Thou changest not, Thy compassions they fail not;
As Thou hast been Thou forever wilt be.

'Great is Thy faithfulness!', 'Great is Thy faithfulness!'
Morning by morning new mercies I see!
All I have needed Thy hand hath provided –
'Great is Thy faithfulness', Lord unto me!

Summer and winter, and springtime and harvest,
Sun, moon and stars in their courses above,
Join with all nature in manifold witness
To Thy great faithfulness, mercy and love.

Pardon for sin and a peace that endureth,
Thy own dear presence to cheer and to guide,
Strength for today and bright hope for tomorrow,
Blessings all mine, with ten thousand beside!

Doubts, fears and anxieties concerning our basic needs in life only betray a fundamental lack of faith (Matt. 6.30). The God who is our Father will never let his children down.

The Lord disciplines those that he loves

Discipline is not a popular concept in today's world. The very mention of the word usually is laced with negative connotations. It is almost invariably associated with punishment for doing wrong and perhaps even brings back painful memories of treatment meted out by a parent or teacher at the end of a cane in days when corporal punishment was the accepted penalty for bad behaviour. It is not surprising, then, that such dark associations are projected – perhaps subconsciously – on to the Bible's teaching in this area. If that is the case, it is a sad distortion of the truth.

The primary thrust in the biblical understanding of discipline is positive, not negative. We see it in the mission statement of the Bible's self-understanding in what Paul says to Timothy in his second epistle. Having declared the divine origin of Scripture, he goes on to outline its fourfold usefulness, the last item on his list being, '…training [or, discipline] in righteousness' (2 Tim. 3.16).[23] The verb he uses comes from the Greek family of words which have given us the English word 'gymnasium' and those words related to it. It is one of those words which paints a picture as it conveys its meaning: the picture of an athlete working out in the gym.

There is a positive, self-imposed discipline which is geared towards personal improvement and general well-being. It is the sportsman accepting a regime of careful diet and regular training in order to reach peak fitness in time for the event. It is the student who resists the temptation to spend her life socialising because she needs a steady pattern of work to pass her course and move on

to something else. It is the wise mother who knows that unless her children are in bed at a reasonable hour each night and follow certain basic house-rules about times for meals, amount of television watched and making time for homework, their little lives will fall apart. This kind of discipline is not punishment – despite what an oarsman on circuit-training might feel! – it is constructive exercise.

So it is with God's children. As they are born into God's family they find a desire to order their lives God's way which was not there before. They will gravitate towards new patterns in life. For some, this will mean abandoning habits that were damaging to themselves and others, perhaps even relinquishing friendships which were less than helpful in terms of their influence. But it is not merely a matter of 'do not...'; in place of what must go, new patterns will be placed. Paul describes this ongoing change in terms of no longer conforming to the fallen world in which we live, but instead being transformed as our minds are renewed by the Word of God (Rom. 12.1-2). There is an inward self-discipline which involves consciously setting both mind and heart on things above (Col. 3.2). There is also an external dimension to this new self-mastery.

In the same way as trainers and tutors play a part in and have their methods for bringing out the best in those under their care, so God applies certain external constraints to aid our spiritual improvement. They are sometimes described as the means of grace and are described helpfully and concisely in the story of the New Testament Church.

After the day of Pentecost, when some 3,000 souls were converted, Luke tells us what those new believers did as they began to find their feet in God's family: 'They

continued steadfastly in the apostles' doctrine and fellowship, in the breaking of bread and of prayers' (Acts 2.42). There, if you like, are the four key exercises in the circuit pattern of God's gym. Several details are worth highlighting.

One is the way in which these early converts committed themselves to these things in a disciplined way. The expression 'continued steadfastly' sounds somewhat archaic, but basically it means that these people devoted themselves to a new pattern of life. There was an underlying commitment which rose above the innate temptation to be spiritually negligent and lazy. There is an immediate lesson there for many Christians in today's *laissez faire* world. Discipleship involves devotion and commitment. In total contrast to the spirit which says, 'Do what you feel like doing and do it when the urge happens to take you', there must be a disciplined approach to living as a Christian. This will impinge upon attitudes in every area of life, both private and public. When we hear of a move away from the time-honoured understanding of a daily devotional life of the believer to a new spirituality, alarm bells ought to ring. It was not mere evangelical or pietistic tradition which canonised the practice of starting and ending the day with God, but rather God himself in his Word (Psalms 1.2-3; 92.1-2). To lose that regular habit is to jeopardise the dynamics of a meaningful relationship with him.

The new Christians we read of in Acts devoted themselves to four particular aspects of church life: the Word (for that is the essence of the apostles' teaching), fellowship, the sacraments and prayer. These are the four necessary components of healthy church life. Whatever

else may be provided by the ecclesiastical calendar and curriculum, these may not be overlooked. Each has its own unique contribution to make in shaping the Christian life of individuals and moulding the body of the Lord's people together as a unit.

The precise value of these elements of congregational life and practice may not be immediately apparent – there will always be things which seem more appealing and spectacular. The Christian world has never had much trouble attracting followers to the latest spiritual spectacular road-show and in an age of rapid communication, the latest fad in one place soon becomes the fashion of the church in the global village. But the self-evident limited shelf-life of these phenomena ought to be an indicator of their deficiencies.

The means of grace prescribed by God in Jerusalem after Pentecost (which were no more than a carry-over from his provision for his people for millennia) have proved themselves more than adequate for successive generations of Christians world-wide. Athletes who depend on anabolic steroids come and go and are forgotten, Christians who depend on the spiritual equivalent suffer the same fate. There is no alternative to healthy discipline in Christian living.

There is a positive dimension to God's discipline, but there is a negative element also. There are indeed occasions when discipline is punishment – Fatherly intervention when there is no other way to restore his wandering children. In fact, the writer to the Hebrews tells us that such treatment from God is evidence that we are his and that he truly loves us.

'My son, do not despise the chastening of the Lord, nor be discouraged when you are rebuked by Him; for whom the Lord loves He chastens, and scourges every son He receives.' If you endure chastening, God deals with you as with sons; for what son is there whom a father does not chasten? But if you are without chastening, of which all have become partakers, then you are illegitimate and not sons (Heb. 12.5-8).

God does not punish because he is capricious or moody – the kind of treatment which was expected from the gods in the Greek and Roman world of the day – but because he loves his children and wants them to be the best as well as have the best.

The threats enshrined in God's covenant (see, for example, Deut. 28.15-68) are never idle threats but are directed first of all towards those who truly belong to God. Sometimes they are enacted through God's providence, as with those who abused the Lord's Supper in Corinth and became ill, several to the point of death (1 Cor. 11.30). On other occasions it falls to those entrusted with the rule of God's household on earth to apply discipline, and, if necessary, actually to exclude from fellowship (Matt. 18.15-18).

Despite the negative overtones of such divine intervention, it has a positive purpose in view. As the passage in Hebrews goes on to indicate:

We have had human fathers who corrected us, and we paid them respect. Shall we not much more be in subjection to the Father of spirits and live? For they

indeed for a few days chastened us as seemed best to them, but He for our profit, that we might be partakers of His holiness. Now no chastening seems to be joyful for the present, but painful, but afterward it yields the peaceable fruit of righteousness to those who have been trained by it (Heb. 12.9-11).

God's goal is quite simply to make his children holy – a prerequisite for fellowship with himself (Heb. 12.14) – and allow them to experience the righteousness and peace that is found in living in communion with him.

We should not, therefore, shrink back from the Lord's punishment. It is not out of keeping with his character as the God of love, but rather a powerful expression of it. The church must always be careful not to allow the distorted, if not perverted, views of discipline which prevail in the secular world to contaminate the biblical picture of how the truly loving Father deals with his much beloved children.

Safeguard against spiritual myopia

When this well-rounded view of what God does as Father for and with his children is achieved, only then can we be preserved from an ever-recurring failure of God's people in the past. In the history of his people in Old Testament times we see a tendency to become taken up with the gift instead of the Giver. When God brought his people out of Egypt into Canaan, he gave them a land of unbelievable wealth and prosperity. But it was never intended as an end in itself, or any kind of substitute for their relationship with him. Yet over and over again, that is precisely what

happened. Thus by the time we reach the period of the Judges we find the recurring cycle of the people turning away from God towards the land and their own interests, God punishing them – often by afflicting the land, their turning back to God in penitence and God restoring to them and to the land the fortunes they had lost. So we find in the Old Testament context that the land becomes a kind of barometer of the spiritual state of the people of God.[24] This trend had continued, even through the ultimate sanction of exile, to the time of Jesus with the notion that the promised Kingdom of God would be some kind of military or political entity.

Thus the church has always been in need of protection from spiritual short-sightedness, a failure to see that it does not exist for self-fulfilment. The good things which are invested in the life of the church are not an end in themselves, but are pointers which direct us towards our God and Father, who is the giver of every good and perfect gift which comes down from above (James 1.17).

7

A Father's Faithfulness

'How can I give you up, Ephraim? How can I hand you over, Israel?' (Hosea 11.8). These are the words God speaks to the people he has just described as the child he loved and 'My son' (Hosea 11.1). They have rebelled against him in the most horrendous way. Their behaviour has been graphically compared to a woman guilty of adultery, persistently spurning the love of her faithful husband who seeks to draw her back to himself. Yet God's heart goes out to them, indeed he goes on to say, 'My heart churns within Me; My sympathy is stirred. I will not execute the fierceness of My anger...' (Hosea 11.8-9). In a most amazing way, God declares his faithfulness to his own people. He will not abandon them.

The language and imagery of family life provides the most potent way in which God could have conveyed the message of the prophecy of Hosea to his people at this time. It is impossible to read the prophet's words (and think of his experiences in this episode) without feeling simultaneously outraged and ashamed. The sense of outrage is there because of the despicable way in which Gomer, the prophet's wife, treated her husband and family. The sense of shame is there because we have all behaved in a similar way in our relationship with God.

Yet as God speaks in that situation through the prophet's

actions towards his own wife and through his ministry to
God's wayward people, the effect is to melt the heart of
even the most hardened backslider. The faithfulness of
God is staggering.

The effect of infidelity is to create instability in
relationships and in family life. This was the case for
Hosea's family. He was left to cope alone with the pressures
of looking after children and home while his wife brought
disgrace upon the family name in the community by her
adulterous behaviour. Fear, anxiety and uncertainty came
flooding into that home. So also on the wider canvas of
the book. The behaviour of those who were guilty of
spiritual adultery in the family of God had destabilised
the complete cross-section of relationships in that context.
In both cases the only factor which prevented complete
disintegration into chaos was the faithfulness of the
respective husbands involved: Hosea and God.

It is the theme and implications of the faithfulness of
God that we now want to examine together in the
relationship between God and his children.

God's unchangeable decree

The roots of God's faithfulness to his children lie in the
unchangeableness of his eternal decree. That is, as God in
his sovereignty has 'foreordained whatsoever comes to
pass',[25] so he guarantees the outcome of what he has
purposed in his will. It is not the law of the Medes and the
Persians 'which does not alter' (Dan. 6.8), but that of
God in heaven. We find this truth at the heart of Paul's
comments on the believer's eternal security and the comfort

which may be derived from that. The life of the believer is bound up with the purposes of God in predestination, not in some clinical detached fashion, but with all the warmth of being brought near to the heart of God as his own adopted children. He tells the Ephesian Christians:

> Just as He chose us in Him [Christ] before the foundation of the world, that we should be holy and without blame before Him in love, having predestined us to adoption as sons by Jesus Christ to Himself, according to the good pleasure of His will (Eph. 1.4-5).[26]

The concept of the believer's experience and destiny being shaped by a distant decision of God's in eternity need not send shivers down our spines, because God's purpose, even at the level of his dealings with individuals, is wrapped up in his unfathomable love.

It is nothing short of tragic that the doctrines of election and predestination have been caricatured by many as scholastic and inimical to warmth in Christian experience. This may be due in part to the way in which these truths have been handled by certain preachers and in certain types of Christian circles. The truths have been wrested from the context in which they are presented in God's Word and turned either into dry academic issues, or else into a battleground between particular groupings within the church and have become a test of orthodoxy. The strange thing is that the Bible itself never handles these truths in that way. They are never found in a polemical context, but rather at the heart of statements which are designed to comfort and encourage God's children.

It is not surprising, then, that they should occur in one

of the great passages in the book of Romans which deals with the issue of assurance of faith and salvation. There Paul underpins his monumental statement about the security of the child of God with the foundational statement that those

> whom He foreknew, He also predestined to be conformed to the image of His Son, that He might be the firstborn among many brethren. Moreover whom He predestined, these He also called; whom He called, these He also justified; and whom He justified, these He also glorified (Rom. 8.29-30).

Paul is simply demonstrating the fact that the entire superstructure of Christian experience and destiny rests upon the unshakeable foundation of what God has decreed in eternity. And, far from being some surreal plan and purpose, its focus is the creation of a new family of God out of the ruins of the fallen family of man.

Such truth is deliberately intended to pull the gaze of the eye of faith away from self and personal ability to God and his unwavering purpose. The practical benefit of this is almost incalculable. So often people waver on the brink of believing, but hold back because they do not trust their own ability to sustain the life of faith in the face of the pressures of a fallen world. The fact is that they could never even begin to do so, even if they wanted to. What God shows us in his Word is the fact that our frail and feeble human actions are undergirded by his mighty sovereign will. Thus the act of faith is not faith in ourselves, but always faith in him and his promise and Word.

There he shows himself as the unchangeable and ever-

faithful God. His faithfulness to himself and to his revelation in Scripture inevitably means faithfulness to his children: those to whom he has made himself known.

God's authenticating seal

God makes himself publicly accountable for what he has decreed and promised. He does so by applying a seal to those who are in Christ Jesus. Paul describes it in these terms:

> In Him you also trusted, after you heard the word of truth, the gospel of your salvation; in whom also, having believed, you were sealed with the Holy Spirit of promise, who is the guarantee of our inheritance until the redemption of the purchased possession, to the praise of His glory (Eph. 1.13-14).

The gift of God's Holy Spirit to everyone who trusts in God's Son serves as an authenticating mark in the lives of those who are God's children.

Despite the wide range of interpretations which have been applied to Paul's statement that the Spirit functions as a seal, it seems best to allow the comment in the following verse to interpret for us what the apostle has in mind: there he writes that the Spirit also functions as a 'guarantee'.[27] When we keep that dimension of this truth in mind it shows that the Holy Spirit serves as the interface between the eternal decree of God – which is inaccessible to the natural mind – and the conscious experience of those who come to faith in Christ.

He thus serves a twofold purpose in this capacity. He

binds God to his own Word and promise and he enables and allows the believer to appropriate that Word and promise for himself and take comfort from it.

The use of seals has become quite rare in the modern world, at least in the everyday sphere, but that was not the case in the world in which Paul was writing. There and then it was commonplace to see seals being used, for example, in the transportation and sale of merchandise. Under those circumstances the seal had a binding effect on the vendor who had applied his seal to his produce; it guaranteed the contents to be all that he claimed them to be. It also had a reassuring effect on the recipient. He could rest assured that his purchase was genuine and if it proved otherwise he had legal recourse against the one who had applied the seal.

Hence the presence and work of the Holy Spirit in the lives of God's children brings home the reality of the faithfulness of God into actual human experience. If you like, it comes off the written page of God's Word and is instead inscribed upon the hearts of those who believe. At times when we are prone to doubt, it is the Spirit who enables us to conquer our doubts and fears, primarily by turning us again to God's promise revealed in his Word and through his Son, but also through dealing with our hearts and minds which continue to be affected by the sin which remains within us.

The Spirit has a ministry of affirmation within God's family which fosters stable living, at both the individual and corporate levels, which rests upon the reliability of the God, who heads the home, and his faithfulness to his Word to his children.

A reason for certainty

When we look at the lives of some of God's most useful servants, whether in the record of Scripture or the history of the church, we cannot but be struck by the measure of certainty they enjoyed in the face of great uncertainty. We could think of biblical figures such as Abraham, Joseph, Moses, Jeremiah, Paul or Timothy. Or we could think of influential characters of church history like Augustine of Hippo, John Calvin, William Carey and many more besides. Their strength and influence were not that of temperament; they did not have an above-average degree of boldness built into their constitution. Indeed the opposite was often the case: some of these people had quiet, retiring dispositions which made them instinctively recoil from hardship and adversity. Yet they persevered against all odds. The secret of their certainty can be found only in their confidence in the faithfulness of God and the fact that God proved himself worthy of such convictions.

The outworking of this confidence is well illustrated in the way Paul builds on his declaration of God's eternal purpose in salvation in Romans and says, at least in part, by way of personal testimony:

Who shall separate us from the love of Christ? Shall tribulation, or distress, or persecution, or famine, or nakedness, or peril, or sword? As it is written, 'For Your sake we are killed all day long; We are accounted as sheep for the slaughter.' Yet in all these things we are more than conquerors through Him who loved us. For I am persuaded that neither death nor life, nor angels nor principalities nor powers, nor things present

nor things to come, nor height nor depth, nor any other created thing, shall be able to separate us from the love of God which is in Christ Jesus our Lord (Rom. 8.35-39).

Paul had personally faced all these obstacles in his Christian life as well as many more (2 Cor. 11.22-33), but as he put his confidence in God, he proved him faithful to his Word and promises. The inward persuasion he is able to testify to in this passage is repeated with added poignancy as the apostle sits on death row in a Roman prison cell awaiting certain execution. There he boldly says:

> I know whom I have believed and am persuaded that he is able to keep what I have committed to him until that Day (2 Tim. 1.12).

Even the prospect of death as a stark and imminent reality could not dislodge Paul's confidence in the God into whose hands he had placed his life.

A conviction about the faithfulness of God is vital if we are to withstand the onslaught on our faith while we continue to live in a hostile world. It is being able to hold on to the truth that God will always hold on to his children which has kept his people from losing their nerve through successive generations of conflict.

A reason to return

Another dimension of the faithfulness of God is found in what he does when his children are unfaithful to him.

This is the issue which lies at the heart of the prophecy of Hosea and this is the issue with which Christians of all generations find themselves grappling in the midst of sin and failure. They seriously wonder if there are indeed grounds for them to return to the God they have failed. The answer is, of course, that they can and must.

Perhaps the best known example of this is found in the life of David and in the words he penned in the twenty-third psalm. It has often been assumed that this must have been composed in David's youth while he was himself a shepherd taking care of his father's sheep. There is a subconscious mental image in the minds of many as they read these idyllic lines of a shepherd boy in the prime of life out on the hills around Bethlehem, musing on the love of God. The reality may well be quite different. There is good reason to believe that this psalm was composed by David, not in the early stages of his life, but towards the end. Thus his reflections take on more robust proportions because they are not musings in abstraction, but rather against the backdrop of a very full and varied life and a very rich experience of God.

So, when we come to the familiar line, 'He restores my soul...' (Psalm 23.3), we are not left wondering what David might be thinking of within the limited experience of a teenager, but rather see an old man who draws enormous comfort from this as he looks back on a life of sin and failure as a child of God. The nadir of his straying, of course, being the episode in which David became an adulterer with Bathsheba and the cold-blooded murderer of her husband Uriah. It was then, more than at any other time in his life, that David discovered the reality of the

God whose faithfulness towers above the unfaithfulness of his erring children. He brings his wandering sheep back into the warmth and security of his fold.

When we alienate ourselves from God, even as his children, we have no warrant to remain in a spiritual wilderness. We are to return to our God, because he is not capricious or unpredictable. He remains true to those who are truly his children and to his unchangeable Word. This was the response evoked by the preaching of Hosea at a time of national straying from God. Although their initial response proved to be premature and superficial, the right sentiment was there when the people said,

> Come and let us return to the LORD; for He has torn, but He will heal us; He has stricken, but He will bind us up. After two days He will revive us; on the third day He will raise us up, that we may live in His sight. Let us know, let us pursue the knowledge of the LORD. His going forth is established as the morning. He will come to us like the rain, like the latter and former rain to the earth (Hosea 6.1-3).

Where there is genuine contrition of heart and recognition of God's faithful mercy, there is full warrant for returning to him in humility to seek forgiveness and restoration. This is precisely how God wants his children to respond to him.

We see it further illustrated in the experience of Peter when he denied the Lord on the evening Jesus was arrested. He had sunk to depths which were arguably deeper than those plumbed by David when he had denied God by his

behaviour. Yet there is full restoration for him. When Peter was with Jesus along with the disciples on the shores of Galilee after the resurrection, John records for us the moving exchange between Jesus and Peter. In this Peter, face to face with Jesus, is brought to acknowledge what he had done and, having denied him three times, now confesses his love for him three times. Jesus then assures Peter of his restoration, not just to fellowship with him, but also to usefulness in his service (John 21.15-19).

Such experiences in the Christian life are inevitably painful and yet God is able to use them to bring us into a deeper relationship with him and a richer appreciation of the fact that it is the faithfulness of God which keeps us as his children and not any inherent faithfulness that we have in ourselves. The Peter who emerged from the denial-restoration episode – who we see in Acts and through his epistles – is markedly different from the one we had come to know in the Gospels. The shame and pain of failure followed by the wonder and joy of being restored fashioned in him a depth of humility and dependence on God which was previously absent.

The danger of presumption

There is of course a danger in all of this. It is possible to misconstrue the Bible's teaching on the faithfulness of God in such a way as to claim an assurance for which there is no warrant. Scripture has many warnings about presuming on the faithfulness of God as well as many examples of those who did, only to find themselves on the wrong side of God's justice.

In the Sermon on the Mount Jesus warns that there will be 'many' on the Day of Judgment who will come to him and say, 'Lord, Lord, have we not prophesied in Your name, cast out demons in Your name and done many wonders in Your name?' But his response to them will be, 'I never knew you; depart from Me you who practise lawlessness!' (Matt. 7.22-23). Although they lay claim to a relationship with Jesus Christ on the basis of spectacular spiritual phenomena, no relationship exists and Christ has no obligation for them.

The same could be said about Judas, who for at least three years saw himself as having an intimate place in the family of God, only to discover too late how far from the truth the reality of his life was. Or those of whom Paul spoke when he met with the Ephesian elders on the beach at Miletus. He warned the leaders of that church that 'from among yourselves men will rise up, speaking perverse things, to draw away the disciples after themselves' (Acts 20.30). Then again there were those mentioned by the apostle John in the latter part of the first century AD who had turned their backs upon the church and the people of God. He refers to such people in strong language, describing them as 'antichrists' who 'went out from us, but they were not of us' (1 John 2.19). At one time they were able to create a most plausible impression of being part of the covenant community and only with the passage of time did the truth about them emerge.

In all of these cases, although the profession of faith of the people involved was ultimately to prove spurious, there was a time when it seemed convincing, even to those in leadership in the church.

The presence of hypocrites among the ranks of the faithful has been a characteristic of the church throughout its history. Referring to Old Testament times and the experience of Israel as the church of that dispensation, Paul says, 'they are not all Israel who are of Israel' (Rom. 9.6). In other words, simply belonging to the people of God through outward association was by no means a guarantee of belonging to God in living spiritual relationship. Jesus drove this point home to the Jews of his day in the confrontation which he had with them over the question of their freedom. When he told them that they needed to be set free through the knowledge of the truth of God through fellowship with the Son of God, they protested that they had never been enslaved in the first place: 'We are Abraham's descendants and have never been in bondage to anyone. How can you say, "You will be made free?"' (John 8.33). They could not see the difference between outward appearance and inward reality.

It is no longer a claim to national identity that people appeal to as a basis for inclusion in the family of God – that was bound up with the unique character of Old Testament Israel as having a national identity as the People of God. But many people still assume that because they have some sort of outward affiliation with the church as the people of God – through baptism, or confirmation perhaps – that this allows them to hold title to a place in heaven.

To live in such presumption is a most dangerous thing, not least because of the chilling words that such people are destined to hear from the Christ they thought they knew: 'I never knew you; depart from Me...' (Matt. 7.23).

Covenant faithfulness

The key to understanding the faithfulness of God is to be found within the framework of his covenant. Paul tells Timothy, in the context of warning against hypocrites and impostors, 'If we are faithless, He remains faithful; He cannot deny himself' (2 Tim. 2.13). This statement has vexed commentators because the general tenor of the statement is one of encouragement: a reminder of the efficacy of Christ's work and the certainty of God's promise for those who believe (2 Tim. 2.11-12). But we cannot escape the negative overtones of what he is saying. It is clear that, 'If we deny Him, He will also deny us' (2 Tim. 2.12), thus it would appear, even in terms of the symmetry of this comment, that the final remark about the faithfulness of God is deliberately intended to alarm those who turn their back on the faith.

Such a comment is but an echo of Old Testament truth about the covenant character of God. He is the God who promises blessing to those who believe, but also the God who threatens cursing against those who do not. His most severe warnings are reserved for those who come within the privileged orbit of his covenant community, either through birth, or some kind of response to his message, only to turn their backs on such privilege and choose, despite all the light they have been given, to go their own way, not God's. For them the faithfulness of God becomes a dreadful thing which seals their doom. As Paul says, God cannot be inconsistent with himself, he is bound by virtue of his own righteousness, to deal with those who have never truly come to believe in his Son and have chosen to remain in their sin.

For those who do believe, the story is different. It is not as though their lives are somehow better or more commendable than those around them, but simply the fact that they have faced up to the reality of sin in their lives and have confessed that sin to God. To them, God is also faithful, 'He is faithful and just to forgive us our sins and to cleanse us from all our unrighteousness' (1 John 1.9). The mark of true saving faith is the fact that it will be persevering faith. It will endure to the end and lead to salvation (Mark 13.13). The very fact that such faith holds on to the promise that God will be faithful to his children, that he will complete the good work he has begun in them (Phil. 1.6), will enable those who are truly his to pick themselves up when they fall, return to him for his pardon and depend afresh on him for the strength to go on.

It is the knowledge that God will never let his children go that will encourage them never to let go of him.

8

Draw Me With the Cords of Love

People have always struggled to comprehend the mechanics of the relationship between a God who is sovereign and human beings who in some meaningful way are responsible agents before him. It is easy to tip the balance of understanding too far in one direction or the other, leading to divine sovereignty which is not total or human responsibility which is merely theoretical. If we endeavour to be truly biblical in our understanding, the balance is retained. The logical tension does not go away, but as we trust the truth of what God has said, we can rest in the confidence that somehow these two truths are simultaneously true, despite the fact that they present themselves as mutually incompatible to our minds. It is one of those circumstances in Scripture where it pays to remember both the limitations and the fallenness of the human mind and to look forward to the day in the world to come when the mists will clear and we shall see things as they really are.

As we attempt to let the Bible shape our understanding of these things, we discover that God does allow us a glimpse of the mechanism which enables the two sides of this relationship to work together. We discover in a most amazing way that this sovereign God does not work in the

lives of his people by detached supernatural *fiat*, but rather by actually engaging them in a personal way. He does not merely confront them with his will, he confronts them with himself.

When we as a family moved from a small rural community to the busy metropolis of London, one of the most striking differences we found was the way in which people dealt with local authorities and institutions. We no longer knew our bank manager – he (or she?) had no face. All transactions were now carried out with a disembodied voice on the other end of a telephone line. When we ran into difficulties over finding a suitable school for one of our children, we found ourselves dealing with a faceless bureaucracy and were constantly passed from one official to another in telephone conversations, none of whom were prepared to promise anything. All local authority was exercised in a detached, de-personalised fashion. The effect was quite de-humanising.

Sadly, in some Christian circles, the prevailing perception of God and how he operates is not very different. He is a God with no face, reduced to a set of abstract attributes, who operates in a way that is remote from the realities of human experience. When that view of God prevails, it is not surprising that it has a significant effect on the kind of 'Christians' it produces. Almost invariably it leads to a de-personalised faith which is shaped more by a code of practice than a living relationship. It is highly deceptive, because the code of practice is God's code of practice as summarised in the Ten Commandments, but it has been excised from the context and relationship in which it was given. Such a legalistic approach to the Law of God

always manages to lift God's commands out of God's covenant and forget what the Westminster Divines rightly highlighted as 'the preface to the Ten Command-ments'.[28] It is only against the background of this statement (Exod. 20.1-2) that the rest of what God says in that chapter can be understood properly. In the preface to the commands he declares himself to be the God who has loved and saved his people; therefore, in light of who he is and what he has done, he summons them to obedience. If they have heard him correctly their response cannot be one of bare legalistic duty, but loving submission to the One who has loved and rescued them.

This, then, sets the pattern for God's *modus operandi* in his dealings with his people and the way in which he expects them to deal with him and with each other. We cannot overlook the fact that the two tables of God's Law, which are filled with 'You shall...' and 'You shall not...' statements, are summarised by two statements which tell us to *love* both God and neighbour. Where such love is absent, John tells us, the soul is dead (1 John 3.14).

If we go back to Hosea once more we see there how love could be described as God's surgical tool by which he operates on the stubborn, sinful hearts of men. Describing the way he nurtured his people in the early stages of their spiritual existence, God says, 'I drew them with gentle cords, with bands of love...' (Hosea 11.4). When they had gone off after the Baals, he had not coerced them back to himself or even made them what he wanted them to be by bare divine command, instead he showed them his love. God depicts himself as a parent down on the floor with his little child – he actually says, 'I stooped

and fed them' (Hosea 11.4) – patiently working with him to win his love and obedience. It is almost beyond comprehension to think that such a great God would humble himself towards such insignificant and undeserving creatures.

When we are confronted with such a loving God, any self-love in ourselves is exploded in all its ugliness. We are turned away from self-gratification towards the One who has loved us far more than we could ever love ourselves and in love has given us more than we could ever hope for in our wildest dreams (Eph. 3.20-21). The response which it ought to evoke from the hearts of God's children is epitomised in what Paul said to the Corinthians, 'You are not your own, for you were bought at a price' (1 Cor. 6.19-20). The price God paid for the redemption of his people – the death of his own dear Son – was the supreme measure of his love for them and the ultimate motive for them to love him.

It is this principle which God consistently applies to the minds and hearts of his children as he reasons with them, weaning them off the world on to himself.

New allegiance

At the heart of God's dealings with his people is the way he persistently impresses upon them the reality of their new allegiance. This is the foundation upon which all ethical demands are built. Paul expresses this in terms of family allegiances in his letter to the Christians at Ephesus. While he is in mid-flow of exhorting the believers to live a life worthy of the calling they have received in Christ

(Eph. 4.1), he appeals to them on the basis of the change in their lives which took place at conversion. He says: 'For you were once darkness, but now you are light in the Lord. Walk as children of light' (Eph. 5.8).

Previously their family allegiance had been with fallen humanity which was 'darkened in its understanding' (Eph. 4.18), but now they belonged to a new family with a new Father. Indeed the significance of that new family orientation is underscored by the fact that they were not just children, but 'dear children' (Eph. 5.1). In their previous family ties, they were caught up with a father who is the very antithesis of love, who never acts in the interests of those under his control; but in God's family things could not be more different.

The magnet in Paul's exhortation lies in the fact that they are loved by God and precious in his sight. He has paid dearly to make them his and they would do well to remember all that was involved in that adoptive transaction.

There are, no doubt, thousands of people in the world who have been unwanted, unloved and abandoned by their natural parents, but adopted by parents who have loved them dearly. Often the stories of such adoptions can be very moving, especially in countries where there is a scarcity of children available for adoption. It is not uncommon for childless couples in such countries to be prepared to travel far and pay dearly – in emotional as well as financial terms – in order to find a child they can love and make their own. And, even though there may be difficulties being an adopted child, such children usually grow up with a deep awareness of how much they are loved; an awareness which is enriched all the more as they discover

what it cost their parents to bring them into their family.

So it should be with the children of God. As they grow in the faith, so they should grow in appreciation of what it cost God to save them. Far from being a straightforward transaction, it cost God the death of his unique Son to bring many sons and daughters to himself. The more they appreciate how much he has given for them, the more they will want to give in response to him. John puts it in a nutshell with the words, 'We love Him because He first loved us' (1 John 4.19).

Since the cross is the supreme demonstration of God's love – no higher price could be paid for their redemption – so the cross lies at the heart of true self-understanding in the lives of God's people. We see this in Paul. It is there in the way he preaches; the cross is the précis of his message (1 Cor. 2.2), but that is only true because the cross is the key to all that he is as a new person in Christ. He says to the Galatians:

> I have been crucified with Christ; it is no longer I who live, but Christ lives in me; and the life I now live in the flesh I live by faith in the Son of God, who loved me and gave Himself for me (Gal. 2.20).

We can almost hear a stunned note in his voice. No matter how often he thought about that great redemptive fact – with all its particularity – it was beyond taking in! Thus Paul persistently brings his readers back to the sufferings of their Saviour only because he persistently brings himself back to those sufferings so that he should never forget what it cost God to deliver him.

Each generation of God's children needs to reflect on this. As soon as the focus of the Christian life begins to shift away from the cross, it is not long before the practice of the Christian life begins to drift as well. Our sense of allegiance to God will be preserved only so long as we have a clear appreciation of his allegiance to us and how that was expressed in the sacrifice of Jesus.

Different life, different lifestyle

Those who have entered this new relationship with God through his Son and who now have a new allegiance, are called to live in a way that is different from their former lifestyle as unbelievers. The ethical demands of this new life flow out of the character of God himself and can be seen in the way that Paul describes Christians as 'children of light' (Eph. 5.8). It is a graphic description which taps into the Bible's use of light as an illustration. The illustration enables the reader to see redemption split into a spectrum of truths which have a bearing on what it means to have been brought into fellowship with God and to live in a way that is fitting for such fellowship.

We can think of it in terms of what God himself is like. John describes him as the God who is light, in whom is no darkness at all (1 John 1.5). He is the God who is the very essence of purity: undefiled and uncontaminated by sin. As the One who is the spiritual head of the home he sets the tone for all who live within the home. Paul certainly has such thoughts in mind when he calls on the Ephesian Christians to 'be imitators of God as dear children' (Eph. 5.1). God himself is to be the pattern for those who belong to him.

When it is construed in such terms, the incentive to pursue that great goal is intensified. It is quite simply the desire of a child to be like his or her father. In our natural homes, where fathers have been what they ought to have been, the children have grown up wanting to emulate their father. His commendable traits have ingrained themselves so deeply in the lives of his children that, subconsciously or otherwise, they want to pattern their lives after his. Of course the same is true of how children relate to their mothers as well. It is not as though a father has the monopoly on all the traits that should be found in children, regardless of their sex, as they grow and develop. So it is with God. Although he is presented in masculine terms in Scripture, it does not mean that God is male. He rises above the attributes of gender and is presented at times as having the kind of qualities that are often associated with motherhood. We see this, for example, in Isaiah, where God compares himself with a mother who cannot forget her child (Isa. 49.15) and a mother who is her child's source of deepest comfort (Isa. 66.13). The more his children come to know him and appreciate him – not least as the One who has loved them with everlasting love (Jer. 31.3) – the more they want to be like him. Christians can live as children of light only insofar as they cultivate fellowship with the God who is light.

Our understanding of this is enhanced when we turn to the use of light imagery in relation to Jesus. He describes himself as 'the Light of the world' (John 8.12), but also describes his followers as 'the light of the world' (Matt. 5.14) as well. Jesus is the very enfleshment of God. If it is difficult for creatures who are flesh and blood to get

their minds around a God who is light and what it means to be like him, that difficulty is removed when they come face to face with Jesus as the incarnate Son of God. 'In him all the fullness of the Godhead dwells bodily' (Col. 2.9). Thus the human face of what we are to pursue is to be found in Christ.

Christians can be 'light' only in a derivative sense as they share in the life of God through his Son and as they consciously model their lives on him by following his commands. When we explore the human dimension of being light as the children of God, particularly in what Jesus says to Nicodemus, we see that the change of life of which Jesus speaks, cannot be divorced from the necessity of a change of heart. Jesus tells the seeking Pharisee that life without God is life which *loves* darkness rather than light (John 3.19) and is reflected in a wicked lifestyle. Before lifestyle can be changed there needs to be nothing short of new life given from above (John 3.3) which will issue in a transfer of our affection from darkness to light: from sin to God. The earliest stirrings of that new life will be the consciousness of being so loved by God that he gave his only begotten Son in order to provide salvation (John 3.16). That awareness leads to new self-understanding and to a completely new direction in life.

True self-image

It is not without significance that it is to a Pharisee that Jesus speaks about God's love for the world and the way it is expressed. The whole mind-set of that religious grouping was conditioned to think in terms of God's loving people on the basis of what he saw in them. Their view is

epitomised in the parable of the Pharisee and the tax collector who went up to the temple to pray (Luke 18.10-14). As the Pharisee spoke to God, his prayer was full of himself and clearly was offered in the assumption that God was bound to be impressed and respond positively to him. He had an inflated impression of himself that failed to grasp the truth about what he was like and how God really saw him.

In total contrast, the tax collector saw himself in such a way as to be filled with shame and not dare to come too near to God. He remains at the back of the temple, unable to bring himself to raise his head in the presence of God and describes himself literally as '*the* sinner' (Luke 18.13). Yet Jesus tells us he was the one who went home justified. This parable says a great deal about how we arrive at true self-appraisal.

It has become popular to talk about self-image and self-worth with the view that all a person needs to have in life in order to succeed is a positive view of themselves. If people can be encouraged to believe in themselves, then a world of opportunity will open up before them in terms of what they can achieve. The key to life for many has become 'the feel-good factor'. So long as they can feel good about themselves and the little world they live in, they can get on in life. In the eycs of some, particularly politicians, this has become the very cement which holds together the fabric of society.

Such an outlook on life raises problems when we face the truth about ourselves and the little world in which we operate. Then we realise that if we are being honest there is little to feel good about. We are full of inconsistency and

failure and we are surrounded by all kinds of greed, cruelty and exploitation. Rather than encouraging us to believe in ourselves and human nature in general, what we see creates a crisis of confidence in humanity.

Yet ironically it is at that point that the Bible tells us a true self-image begins. Our self-worth is not to be found in what we are by nature, but in what we become through faith in Jesus Christ. It is only when we are brought into a living, loving relationship with God through him that we start to appreciate ourselves truly. Once more it is the apostle Paul who well exemplifies what this change of outlook means.

Paul quite frequently makes reference to his past and to his religious pedigree. In the Jewish world the latter was almost as enviable as his Roman citizenship in the wider sphere. In fact, putting the two together, Paul had everything going for him as a Jewish Pharisee, schooled to the highest level, with Roman citizenship as well. It is not perhaps surprising that he was dogged by a sinful pride, even as a Christian, which was a lingering hangover from his previous way of life. As he says himself, he had every reason to be confident in the flesh (Phil. 3.4-6). The amazing thing is that he casts all that aside. Indeed he resorts to pretty strong language to describe the value he now places upon what he had been and had achieved in the days before his conversion: the Authorised Version captures something of the bluntness of it in the words, 'I count them but dung' (Phil. 3.8) – even that retains a measure of decorum for English readers!

Paul's pride in himself is summed up in the pride of what he is in Christ. He can say:

Yet indeed I also count all things loss for the excellence of the knowledge of Christ Jesus my Lord, for whom I have suffered the loss of all things (Phil. 3.8).

Thus the whole orientation of his life becomes Christ-ward in a way that colours his entire existence. For him, to live was Christ (Phil. 1.21) – his life in its totality was wrapped up with Jesus. For him, death was gain, a fact that led him to look forward, with irrepressible eagerness, to the day when he would see his Lord and Saviour face to face (Phil. 3.13-14). Paul knew full well that true fullness of life can be found only in union and communion with Jesus.

It is that radical new self-awareness that every Christian must cultivate if he or she is going to begin to discover their God-given potential in life. It is not enough to pay lip-service in a passive way to the fact that as Christians we are 'in Christ'; there must be a deliberate, self-conscious effort to make that the controlling factor of how we live. It is only as we live consciously in the light of this new relationship that our lifestyle will change. We ought to be able to echo the great confession of Paul: 'It is no longer I who live, but Christ who lives within me; and the life which I now live in the flesh, I live by faith in the Son of God' (Gal. 2.20).

We relate to Jesus, not just as the One who alone can enable us to live for God, but as the One who is the perfect model of what it means to live for God. We see in the incarnate Christ a most amazing voluntary subordination to the will of the Father; a submission that was not required of him and which in no sense reflected inferiority within

the Godhead. But as perfect man and true representation of what it means to be human, he willingly and gladly submitted to the will of God. The mainspring of this obedience was his love for the Father. It is anticipated in the Psalms by the statement, 'I delight to do Your will, O my God, and Your law is within my heart' (Psalm 40.8). It is fulfilled in the words of Jesus himself as he spoke with his disciples, 'I do not seek My own will, but the will of the Father who sent Me' (John 5.30). The perfect relationship between Father and Son is manifest in perfect obedience. So for all who are children of God through faith in Jesus Christ.

'Solid joys and lasting treasures...'

It was in the solemn context of his last discourse with his disciples, on the eve of his arrest and crucifixion, that Jesus brought the essence of his relationship with his followers into sharp focus. He says quite simply, 'If you love me, keep my commandments' (John 14.15). Further on he develops the thought by saying:

> If you keep My commandments, you will abide in My love, just as I have kept My Father's commandments and abide in His love' (John 15.10).

There he makes it clear that those who are in fellowship with him must model their fellowship on the fellowship that exists between the Father and the Son.

There is no question but that this is a costly pattern to follow. To submit to the will of God means that we must deny the will of the world and of self. There is sacrifice

involved in obedience. We are perhaps inclined to get alarmed by the scale of sacrifice involved when we view it in purely personal terms; but whatever personal cost we may incur through obedience to God, it is nothing in comparison with the sacrifice made by Jesus as he subjected himself to the will of the Father.

Although such sacrifice is costly, it is by no means without its reward. The writer to the Hebrews also marries the obedience of Christ to the obedience of his children when he holds up Jesus as the supreme model of perseverance and the supreme incentive to persevere (Heb. 12.1-3). Of the prospect of the sacrifice on Calvary, he says:

Who for the joy that was set before Him endured the cross, despising the shame and has sat down at the right hand of the throne of God (Heb. 12.2).

To use the language of Isaiah, Jesus would 'see the labour of His soul and be satisfied' (Isa. 53.11). On the other side of the cost of sacrifice was the benefit that would flow from it. Although there is a distinction to be drawn between the nature of the benefits of Christ's sacrifice, in that they are redemptive, and those of the sacrifices made by believers, the connection is clearly there.

Jesus speaks of the life of discipleship as the life of self-denial and cross-bearing (Mark 8.34). The obedience he required of his followers would be costly. He was to spell out its cost in graphic detail in terms of lost property and losses in family life (Mark 10.29). However the gains vastly outweigh the losses. He goes on to describe not only the eternal rewards of his children, but also those

which they will experience in the here and now (Mark 10.30). This perspective allowed Paul to rise above his present sufferings and regard them as not worth comparing to what would be his when Jesus ultimately appears (Rom. 8.18).

There are indeed joys and pleasures which are on offer in this present world and which preoccupy the time and energies of the vast proportion of humanity. But John Newton was right when he wrote:

> Fading is the worldling's pleasure,
> All his boasted pomp and show;
> Solid joys and lasting treasure
> None but Zion's children know.

'Fullness of joy' and 'pleasures for evermore' are to be found nowhere else but at the right hand and in the presence of God (Psalm 16.11). There is joy in obedience because obedience deepens the loving bond between God and his children. The Father does not coerce us into submission, rather he woos us by his tender love and care and ever holds before us the joy that will be ours on the other side of sacrifice.

9

My Brother's Keeper

It should not surprise us that being brought into a new relationship with God through Jesus Christ also means that we are brought into new relationships with those around us, especially those who also belong to the family of God. This is helpfully summarised in chapter 26 of *The Westminster Confession of Faith*, which is entitled, 'Of Communion of Saints'. It opens with a statement to the effect that those who are united to Christ and enjoy fellowship with him are likewise united to each other in him and enjoy communion with each other.[29]

As we begin to explore this aspect of life in God's family, we find ourselves being taken back to the events surrounding the early days of the human race, recorded in the book of Genesis. There, as we have noted already, one of the first results of the fall was the loss of the sense of community among the embryonic race. The relationship between Adam and Eve was damaged, as became clear when God confronted them, and it is not long before we discover other relationships being impaired as well.

Cain and Abel argue, come to blows and the younger brother becomes the first murder victim of history. God once more confronts the offending party. As he enquires from Cain regarding the whereabouts of Abel, Cain

147

protests, 'Am I my brother's keeper?' (Gen. 4.9). The raw nerve which God had touched as he started his cross-examination was of course the fact that Cain knew full well that he was. There was an in-built responsibility to the blood relationship that made them members of the same family.

The destructive influence of sin on human relationships has been the story of the human race. From the natural family right up to the global village, successive generations have neglected and abused their responsibility to their fellow men. The human family is a broken family.

The beauty of what God has done in Christ is not merely the *de facto* restoration of relationships through union with his Son, but the practical outworking of this in the daily workings of his family. God lays a responsibility (the *Westminster Confession* describes it as obligation)[30] upon his people to mend the relationships sin has fractured. This has a number of important implications.

No islands in God's family

The first implication is surely that Christians were never intended to exist in isolation: there are no islands in God's family. When vast numbers of people were converted on the Day of Pentecost, they did not merely disperse to their respective isolated backgrounds. We are told that almost immediately they began to meet together on a regular basis (Acts 2.42). This was all the more interesting because the crowd that day was a most diverse assembly (Acts 2.7-11). Whereas there was a natural inclination to go their separate ways or gravitate towards their own particu-

lar grouping, they actually gathered together as one new and diverse family.

This plurality within the family of God is evident throughout the New Testament period, indeed it is seen as something which was a necessity for the life of the church. At times when the yawning chasm between converts from a Jewish background and those who were Gentiles seemed on the verge of splitting the Church, special efforts were made to ensure this did not happen (see, for example, Acts 15.1-29). The same concern for an embracive spirit within God's family comes out again towards the end of the New Testament period, this time in relation to class distinction, in the epistle of James. There James condemns churches which show favouritism to those who attend their meetings on the basis of their material prosperity.

The need for such diversity has always needed to be re-addressed in the history of the church. All too often, perhaps especially within the evangelical wing of the church, there has been a tendency to subdivide the household of faith into a variety of spiritual ghettos. Sometimes it has been class division, sometimes virtual discrimination through ministry which is geared towards the educated and is inaccessible to those who are not. There have been racial and cultural prejudices which have turned congregations into particular ethnic groupings where outsiders are not really welcome. Such a parochial spirit at any level in church life is not only alarming, it is positively unbiblical. Perhaps the most concerning thing of all in recent years is the emergence of a whole body of literature which actually promotes such sub-dividing of

the church as an acceptable means of promoting evangelical church growth.[31]

The entire cross-section of the human family ought to and must be reflected in the cross-section of the redeemed family of God.

If it is wrong to have spiritual islands in the sense of ecclesiastical sub-groupings, it is equally wrong to have such in the sense of individuals who feel free to isolate themselves from wider fellowship with other Christian people. Such a mentality has been on the increase over the past hundred years or so of church life, because of an unbalanced emphasis on personal salvation from a purely personal Saviour. The sense of being part of a Christian community has been all but lost.

In recent times this has been fuelled by a characteristic of Post-modernism which promotes individualism. The 'Swinging Sixties' saw the beginning of revolt against the expected norms of society. People were actively encouraged to 'do their own thing'. Not surprisingly, this attitude soon started to filter through to church life. It surfaces in a general reluctance to be committed to a local congregation, to feel accountable either to leaders in the church, or even to other church members. It leads inevitably to serious problems in the practical exercise of ministry in the church.

It usually coincides with a strongly subjective view of the Christian life: privatised spirituality, refusal to allow others to be involved in seeking God's direction, and an unwillingness to conform, even to recognised biblical standards. Such an outlook is seriously at odds with what God says about the nature of salvation. It is in its very

essence corporate as well as personal and any attempt to excise the corporate element will have a profound impact upon the enjoyment of God's grace in this present world.

There can be no place for individualism among God's people because we can never extricate ourselves from a responsible relationship with everyone else who has been united to Christ through faith. When it says, 'God sets the solitary in families' (Psalm 68.6), it is at least in part a pointer to local expressions of his wider family, where the needs of our spiritual loneliness can be met.

Family fellowship

Families are not just functional, they are existential. They are not merely concerned with *doing* things together, but also with *being* something together and finding great pleasure in that sense of oneness. This lies at the heart of true Christian fellowship. It is nothing less than a shared life – the life of God shared by the children of Adam. It was this corporate participation in God-given life which animated the early gatherings in Jerusalem after Pentecost (Acts 2.42). It was not a common set of interests which brought this rainbow alliance together, nor even a corporate decision to do certain things together, no matter how worthy they might be. Rather it was that they had become something together: the children of God. There was a new-found affinity which drew them out of their natural diversity into a glorious unity. Fellowship existed by virtue of their being in fellowship with Christ, and as fellowship with the Saviour needed to be cultivated, so did fellowship with one another.

Thus the outworking of this new relationship was found

through actually meeting together and engaging in the kind of activities which were conducive to spiritual growth and edification.

Often the significance of simply 'being there' at the stated meetings for public worship and corporate prayer can be missed. Yet when spiritual absenteeism started to become a problem among the believers addressed in Hebrews, the writer had to urge them not to forsake assembling together (Heb. 10.23). Occasional lapses in attendance may be quite legitimate and understandable, in the same way as a son or daughter's being absent from the meal table from time to time may be; but when it becomes a pattern it becomes a problem. Not just a problem for the individual in that it deprives him or her of much-needed spiritual nourishment, but also much-needed contact with fellow believers.

The illustration given to generations of young people's groups of coals in the grate as a picture of Christian fellowship may be well worn, but it is certainly not worn out. If you take a single piece of coal out of a brightly burning fire and place it on the hearth by itself, it is not long before it starts to grow cold and becomes but a dully glowing ember on the hearth, devoid of warmth and usefulness. Take a Christian out of regular fellowship with other Christians and it is not long before his spiritual vitality and usefulness are virtually extinct. Quite simply, we need each other.

Being a family must of course involve functioning as a family. The New Testament identifies many areas in which this family relationship shapes and moulds the way in which we relate to other people in the faith.

There will always be a ministry of encouragement. Some had a particular gift in this area; Barnabas – a nickname meaning 'Son of Encouragement' – was a prime example in the book of Acts (Acts 4.36). Not only was he a large-hearted individual, willing to share what he had with those who were less well off (Acts 4.37), but also he was ever eager to believe the best of others and persuade people to learn from his generous spirit. When the newly converted Paul was under suspicion among the Christians in Jerusalem, it was Barnabas who persuaded them to welcome him as a true brother in Christ (Acts 9.27). Then when Paul's gifts and abilities began to eclipse those of Barnabas, the latter was perfectly happy to stand aside to allow Paul's ministry to blossom in Antioch and then on his missionary journeys.

This ability to encourage is not, however, restricted to specialists; it must be built in to the ministry of all of God's children. In Hebrews 10:24 we are told to so relate to one another in such a way that we might be the stimulus for 'love and good works'. In other words our relationships within the Body of Christ ought to be the catalyst for godly living. That is quite a sobering thought since, if truth be told, the experience of many congregations seems to be that Christians bring out the worst in each other, rather than the best. Peter makes a comment in a similar vein when he says:

Since you have purified your souls in obeying the truth through the Spirit in sincere love of the brethren, love one another fervently with a pure heart (1 Peter 1.22).

The cement which keeps God's family bound together is

the love which translates into action in our daily relationships with each other.

It has been one of the great tragedies of the twentieth century that the currency of love has been completely devalued. Thus when many contemporary Christians read this comment in Peter, they think of it in merely emotional terms. That is problematic in the extreme, because even in the Christian family there are brothers and sisters who manage only to arouse negative feelings in those around them. How, then, does deep, pure love relate to them? The answer is, of course, that the kind of love Peter had in mind embraced more than heart feelings; it involved the mind in deliberate recognition of worth and the will in conscious determination to relate.

Paul describes in more detail what is involved in such loving relationships between God's children in his celebrated passage in Corinthians (1 Cor. 13.1-13). He was not setting out in these verses, as people sometimes mistakenly imagine, to give a neat, detached definition of love, but rather he was responding quite robustly to the lovelessness of the Christians in Corinth. Those who first read these lines in that congregation would have blushed with shame, because those things which Paul condemned they were guilty of, and those things which Paul commended were absent from their lives and fellowship. It just so happens that the Corinthian problem at the heart of church fellowship is much more widespread than we might care to admit. Thus Paul's comments are much more relevant than perhaps we imagine and they come home to us with the same force of rebuke as they did to the original readers in the ancient church.

If our churches were filled with people who displayed the spirit and qualities of these verses, they would be pleasant spiritual homes for God's people. We desperately need people who are patient and kind, not always looking enviously at others. People who are not full of themselves or their own theology, always making their presence felt, as opposed to the presence of their Saviour. A proud disposition like that frequently goes hand in hand with a string of negative attitudes towards other people. Such people are almost invariably rude and hopelessly self-centred, seemingly incapable of listening with any degree of sensitivity to the needs of others. They live life on a short fuse, are quick to respond aggressively under provocation and seem to prefer thinking the worst about others instead of the best, and take perverse delight when their worst suspicions are proved true. They revel in the sins and failures of their brethren. It is strange how truth and virtue do not excite them in the same way. Genuine love is protective, trusting, full of hope and capable of enduring under pressure, and all who claim to belong to God must aspire to that.

The outworking of that kind of love will have an enormous impact on those who struggle under the burdens of life and even those who appear to have collapsed completely.

Love under duress

Christians, especially those who are conservative in their theology, have often been at their weakest when confronted with brothers and sisters who genuinely struggle under the difficulties of life and in particular with those who

have caved in under pressure. These are two areas where relationships within the spiritual family are crucial and biblical love needs to be seen in action.

Paul tells the Galatians that they must 'Bear one another's burdens and so fulfil the law of Christ' (Gal. 6.1). It is only as we turn that statement round and appreciate what it means to fulfil the law of Christ that we will understand what is involved in burden-bearing. Some have suggested that 'the law of Christ' is simply Paul's way of referring to the whole corpus of Christ's instruction, but perhaps he is actually referring to one cardinal detail of that instruction which has a tendency to be overlooked by those who are theologically-minded. Could it not be a subtle reference to Jesus' memorably simple dictum in the Upper Room, 'A new commandment I give to you, that you love one another; as I have loved you, that you also love one another' (John 13.34).

The force of that statement is quite staggering. Jesus was not saying anything new in the sense that the command to love was new: the second table of the law was encapsulated by the words, 'Love your neighbour as yourself' (Matt. 22.39). The newness of his command lay in the paradigm for love that was built into it, namely, Christ's love for his people. The implication Jesus goes on to spell out to the disciples is equally breath-taking: 'By this all will know that you are My disciples, if you have love for one another' (John 13.35). The hallmark of discipleship was to be found in transformed hearts and transformed relationships. The truth of this has often been proved in church experience by its converse. It has been the manifest lack of love in the way professing Christians

deal with each other that has too often become the distinguishing characteristic of the church. There is maybe more truth than we imagine in the jibe that the church is the only army in the world that shoots its wounded! We too easily discredit the gospel and the name of Christ by the way we treat our brothers and sisters before the watching world.

How then does this translate into practice when we see another member of God's family struggling under the pressures of life? Well, at its most basic level it must mean having an eye for others and their needs as well as ourselves and our own. This wider awareness will at least alert us to believers who are in difficulty and should also help us to develop an instinct for them. It requires of necessity a sensitive approach. The temptation is always to assume we know the nature of the need before we have taken time to listen to the person who actually lives with it! That can often take time, as real needs can be buried under layers of other issues which need to be peeled away before the root of the problem is exposed. Even at that stage it is necessary to proceed with care and sensitivity. The term 'heavy shepherding' has been coined as a description of those church leaders who hand out dogmatic prescription solutions to the struggling members of their flock without any real regard for personal circumstances. The true shepherd, like the Good Shepherd, will know his sheep by name (John 10.3, 14, 27) with all the individuality represented by a name. The precise response to any individual will be literally tailor-made for his or her situation.

At times it will be appropriate to take very practical

steps to help as well as simply administering advice and instruction. God dealt with a depressed prophet by giving him a rest and a holiday (1 Kings 19.3-9); similarly the simple step of relieving someone's pressures can be the first step to resolving the problem. The single mother struggling to bring up a lively little family will perhaps need no more than an extra pair of hands or a baby-sitter once a week to give her room to breathe and get her life back into perspective again. And when it comes to her involvement in the life of the church, there is no point telling her she needs to be at the means of grace if no-one is prepared to take practical steps to let her get there!

Such involvement with the needs of others can become prolonged and demanding, both on time and energy. So Paul enters a caveat a little further on to ensure that needy Christians do not become spiritual sponges – always dependant and never able to stand alone. Paul says, 'Each one shall bear his own load' (Gal. 6.5). As one aspect of the fruit of the Spirit is self-control (Gal. 5.23), when it comes to terms of personal spirituality, every child of God needs to be able to stand on his or her own two feet. The goal of individuals and the goal of those who help them as they work through problems is to enable them to cope alone – alone in the sense of being Spirit-filled Christians.

Problems in the Christian life may be one thing, but sin and failure are another. Many who have given in to temptation, especially in a public way, become spiritual cripples and pariahs in the church community. Indeed, it is often deemed to be the most spiritual thing to ostracise such brothers and sisters. We can never be content with that.

Paul sets out the truly spiritual response to such situa-

tions even before he has anything to say about the issue of the ordinary problems and pressures of life. 'Brethren, if any man is overtaken in any trespass, you who are spiritual restore such a one in a spirit of gentleness, considering yourself lest you also be tempted' (Gal. 6.1). The same truth is echoed by James speaking at a slightly later point in early church history when error as well as immorality was becoming a problem to many congregations. 'Brethren, if anyone among you wanders from the truth, and someone turns him back, let him know that he who turns a sinner from the error of his way will save a soul from death and cover a multitude of sins' (James 5.19-20).

The issue at stake is crucial. The objective in dealing with such people is restoration, not retribution. Although an element of punitive discipline may well be appropriate in such circumstances, punishment is not an end in itself. It is for the Lord to dispense ultimate justice and for the church to pray and labour for the evidence of present grace. When Christ himself gives the blueprint for handling sin and failure in the life of the church (Matt. 18.15-20), he too makes it clear that the goal of the exercise is to win a brother over.

There is to be a Christ-like gentleness in the handling of such matters, but a gentleness which does not preclude firmness at the same time. This characteristic is wonderfully illustrated in the way that Jesus responds to the woman caught in the act of adultery (John 8.1-12). She is flabbergasted by his attitude which shows such obvious love for her without for a moment condoning what she has done. She was not required to do some kind of

evangelical penance before she could be restored to the community of the faithful – her public acknowledgment of her sin was sufficient in itself – she simply was told to go and sin no more. One cannot help but notice that when Jesus told her accusers that the person without sin should be the first to cast a stone, the oldest members of the group were the first to slip away (John 8.9). They saw something of themselves in this poor woman and realised that they could so easily have been in her situation if they had been given opportunity to sin, or even, perhaps, if their sin had ever been discovered.

The crucial thing is to bring an erring brother or sister to the point where they acknowledge their sin (see Psalm 32.5). That first means facing the reality of sin in personal terms. There is no point in trying to cover up sin, or call it something else – such measures amount to self-delusion (1 John 1.10). Sin must be recognised for what it is. This will of necessity mean facing up to it before God. He is the offended party in the ultimate sense and to him above all others we are accountable. But there is also the further dimension of facing up to the effects of our sin at the purely human level. There will be those we have sinned against directly, by word or deed, and reparation needs to be made towards them. There will also be those who have been affected indirectly, who will have been let down, or hurt. A measure of public acknowledgment of sin is appropriate towards them as well. It need not necessarily mean a public statement in the sense of having to stand before an assembled congregation, but it must mean going to the affected parties and resolving issues with them.

The outcome of such an exercise will be of benefit not

only to the individual concerned, or even just for the wider well-being of the fellowship to which they may belong. Ultimately the outcome will impinge upon the honour of God himself and the credibility of his gospel.

A wider circle of love

A happy, loving family can be a real gem in any community: a source of help and encouragement to those who are touched by its influence, a model to those who admire its example. The benefits enjoyed by family members themselves spill over in ever widening circles to those who come in contact with them. So it is and should be with the family of God.

Paul develops his instruction to the Galatian churches by saying, 'Therefore, as we have opportunity, let us do good to all, especially to those who are of the household of faith' (Gal. 6.10). He has already elaborated on what it means to do good to the household of faith, but is reminding those who belong to that household that the 'my brother's keeper' principle extends beyond the Christian family to the human family at large.

Once more we find Jesus as the perfect model of what this should entail. He was and is the supreme evangelist who saw his mission on earth as being primarily to preach (Mark 1.38), but this did not preclude a ministry of mercy. He was involved in feeding the hungry, healing the sick, liberating the captives and comforting the lonely. It is perhaps worth noting that this element of his ministry had no strings attached. There is no reason to believe that all who received benefit through healing, feeding, or what-

ever, were necessarily converted. Indeed the apparent smallness of the pre-Pentecost church would tend to suggest that very few of the multitudes actually became disciples. Nevertheless, Jesus pursued that work to the very end and commended it to the disciples as part of the continuing work of the church (Matt. 25.34-40). The presence of hunger, loneliness, sickness and death in the world is the consequence of sin; thus the duty of the church to alleviate such needs is but a part of its wider mandate to wage war on the world, the flesh and the devil through a gospel of Word and deed.

In some ways the shape of this kind of ministry, at least in the western world, has changed as far as the church is concerned. Whereas in past generations it was the church which spearheaded the provision of social, medical and educational care for the wider community,[32] many of these functions have now been taken over by the State or by secular institutions. This has led some to conclude that this practical dimension to the church's mission to the world no longer exists, except perhaps in an overseas missionary context in developing countries. It would be dangerous to begin to think that way because no State or institution can ever adequately meet the enormous needs presented in the care of a nation. One only has to look at Britain and America, both of which owe a great deal to Christian influence in the way national institutions have been shaped, to realise that medical care, social welfare and general education are all in various stages of melt-down. More and more people are becoming the quiet casualties of the system and no amount of government officers can hope to be there to pick up the pieces. Thus it

falls increasingly to community-based churches to recognise these needs and, within the confines of their resources, minister to them. As with their Lord, God's people should not see such provision of care being made conditional upon profession of faith, any more than we would make the free offer of the gospel conditional to a guaranteed response.

When this care is dispensed locally in conjunction with the proclamation of the gospel, the church in the community becomes the training ground for global missionary concern and a recruiting station for those who are called and equipped to serve overseas. It is tempting to see a connection between the decline in concern for local outreach in the terms we have described and the decline in foreign missions and slow-down in the number of people coming forward as missionary candidates. The fact that the mission of the church began at Jerusalem and spread to the ends of the earth (Acts 1.8) not only enshrines history, but also enshrines principle: the model which should shape the witness of the church in every age.

As God's people recognise what it means to be 'my brother's keeper', both within the confines of their own spiritual family and in the wider context of the community, both local and global, they provide a unique window on the gospel of our Lord Jesus Christ. The unbelieving world can see as well as hear the truth of new life through God's Son. Where such love is absent, the opposite is true and the gospel is torpedoed.

10

'Where I am, You May be Also'

I remember a few years ago sitting in our car as we were getting ready to pull out of a French campsite near St Malo at the end of a three week holiday. The radio was on and as we were about to set off, the old 60s' song, 'I'm Going Home', began to play. We had enjoyed a wonderful holiday, but the sentiment of the song well expressed the sentiment of our hearts at that point: we too 'were going home'. For almost a month 'home' had been a tent and we had moved from place to place, soon we would be back where we belonged.

The spiritual overtones of that little episode were not lost on me, even at the time, not least because of the way the Bible talks of life in this world in terms of living in a tent and our being just travellers passing through. For those who are God's children, there is a deep, mysterious longing to go to our everlasting home in heaven. That longing for a true and lasting home was captured in song in the words of an old Negro spiritual which was popularised in many youth groups during the early 1970s in Britain. Those who composed and sang this song originally, far from home and enslaved as they were in America, must have felt an added poignancy in what they sang because their personal circumstances accentuated the biblical truths which they were putting to music:

> This world is not my home, I'm just a-passing through,
> My treasures are laid up somewhere beyond the blue.
> My Saviour beckons me from that far golden shore,
> And I can't feel at home in this world any more.

Those slaves knew they could not return to their home on earth, but through salvation could look forward to a better home above.

The simple fact of life in God's family is that it can never be completely fulfilled here and now. The full enjoyment of all that the Father has planned for us, the Son has purchased for us and the Spirit imparts to us will be ours only in eternity to come. It is vitally important to get these things in perspective, because if we fail, it will have a dreadfully damaging effect on our understanding of the gospel and the kind of aspirations we have for the Christian life. There have been many occasions through the history of the Christian church, not least in recent times, when there has been a lack of balance and God's people have lost their way. In its extremes this tendency has swung between a pietistic other-worldliness and a fixation with the 'here and now'. Getting back on course means rediscovering the well-rounded teaching that we have in the Bible, especially in the New Testament, which will simply prepare us to know what to expect. As we begin to explore this sphere, it helps to bring the relationships between life and death, time and eternity into their proper perspective. It is to this area of God's instruction that we must finally turn.

Living with tension

There is an underlying tension in human existence which we have referred to already.[33] In one sense this tension is resolved through conversion, but in another sense it is not. It is resolved in the sense that Christ gives us the assurance that the deepest needs of the soul are met by him and in him. It is not resolved in the sense that we cannot actually experience his provision to the full until the consummation of all things at his return. Thus the longing that pervades the entire created order for the final appearing of Jesus Christ when he comes again and ushers in the renewal of all things (Rom. 8.22-23). Paul describes this longing in these verses as being like a woman in labour, about to give birth. She cannot breathe her final sigh of relief until her child has been safely delivered.

So it is with God's children. We will not experience complete, pervasive and permanent relief until the eyes of our resurrection body first blink in the sunshine of the new heavens and the new earth and we inhale the first lung-fulls of air in that completely renovated order. Until then there must be tension within our souls. Although at times it will be hard to understand and perhaps even painful to bear, to understand it is to begin to be able to cope with it. The New Testament gives us several helpful angles from which to view this condition and appreciate it in a wider context.

Jesus describes it in terms of being *in* the world, but not *of* the world (John 17.11-14). Indeed he compares his disciples to himself in saying that although he had come into the world, had taken a real human nature to himself and lived among men, he did not belong to that fallen

order, he belonged to the realm of glory. He himself experienced the tension of living effectively as an intruder in an environment which was fundamentally opposed to all that he was and everything he represented. John makes much of this antipathy as he reflects on the coming of Christ in his Gospel. He was not recognised by the world he had made, nor received by the people he had chosen to be his own (John 1.10-11). He came as the light of the world, but sinful men and women preferred their spiritual darkness to being in the light of his presence and Word (John 3.19).

The painful reality of this for Jesus, not just as Son of God and Son of Man, but also significantly as true and perfect man, was experienced at almost every turn during his life on earth. The prophetic truth of Isaiah's words that he would be despised and rejected, with grief and suffering his closest companions (Isa. 53.3), was all too evident. Even though he was the man who went about doing good to all, he was constantly under suspicion and attack, often the object of false accusation and finally, from a human perspective, the victim of a malicious plot. The perfection of Jesus did not for a moment mean that he had an easy or a comfortable life on earth. If that was to be his experience, his disciples had no reason to expect anything different.

Paul takes up the same theme, but puts a slightly different gloss on it. Speaking by way of personal testimony he says, 'For our citizenship is in heaven...' (Phil. 3.20). He had been describing to the Philippians his own personal struggle as a Christian, indicating the many and various ways in which this tension of being torn between two worlds

surfaces in the experience of God's children.

In his memorable statement in the early part of the letter he declares, 'For me, to live is Christ, and to die is gain ... I am hard pressed between the two, having a desire to depart and be with Christ which is better by far' (Phil. 1.21-23). It was not merely the contrast between the fallen world and the perfect world that he had in view, but rather the existence of the redeemed in both. Even in this sinful world he could testify to a transformed existence, which he had come to enjoy through union with his Saviour. But glorious as this was, it simply was not worth comparing to the life he anticipated with Christ in glory.

Paul revels in the righteousness he has found in Christ (Phil. 3.9), nothing in all human experience can compare to this gift which gives him the right to fellowship with God. But that is not all. Justification is inseparably linked to the power of the resurrection of Christ which progressively leads the apostle and indeed all God's children into living conformity to Jesus, a process which will not be complete until the resurrection of the saints (Phil. 3.10-11). Paul is the first to confess that he is far from reaching this goal in his life and experience (Phil. 3.12), and uses the language of struggle to describe his efforts to move closer to his God-given goal (Phil. 3.14-15).

This is the struggle of growing in grace, the tension of sanctification, knowing what we ought to be, but realising how far short we fall of that perfect ideal. It is a living tension that Paul felt keenly in his own walk with God (Rom. 7.7-24). It is precisely the same experience that every child of God will go through as long as he or she remains in the flesh.

In another place in Romans Paul describes the tension from the point of view of living with suffering (Rom. 8.18). There is a very real 'present suffering' which the Christian must endure because he or she lives in a world ravaged by suffering, but there is a 'glory that will be revealed' which belongs to a coming age. Paul wants his believing readers to face this reality and draw comfort from it, that they might be able to hold on in the present by looking forward to what God had prepared for them in the future. In many ways it was an echo of an Old Testament sentiment expressed poetically in the Psalms: 'Weeping may endure for a night, but joy comes in the morning' (Psalm 30.5). The child of God can look forward with hope and confidence to the dawn of God's new day in God's perfect world.

It is, of course, at this point where so much contemporary gospel preaching has been misleading. Preachers have blithely promised that those who come to Jesus can look forward to a trouble-free life, some even daring to claim that God will demonstrate his favour towards his children by making them healthy and wealthy. But attractive as such a message may seem and effective as it might prove in terms of winning 'converts', it is neither faithful to God's Word nor fair to those who respond to it. Such preaching can lead only to a string of cynical casualties who have believed, only to be disappointed and let down, bringing the Name of God into disrepute before a watching world.

That kind of message was certainly not preached by New Testament evangelists, nor was such a life experienced by New Testament Christians. Peter described the

followers of Jesus as pilgrims or strangers scattered throughout the known world (1 Peter 1.1). James had used similar descriptive language at the beginning of his general epistle. Both authors were picking up on the language of the Exodus, showing that the people of God in the days of Moses were destined to a life of travelling through hostile territory, so the people of God in every generation would always be passing through a hostile world. They were resident aliens.

The expression 'resident alien' hit me with some force when I arrived in the United States at the beginning of a three-year stay while I was at seminary there. I had just come through passport control and the immigration officer had examined my documents, stamped my visa and handed it back to me with the words 'resident alien' emblazoned across it! That is what I was in the eyes of the American authorities – an alien, a foreigner who was living temporarily in their country. Often that was precisely how I felt. I knew I did not belong. My culture was different from that of my American neighbours. My heart was somewhere else and I looked forward to the day when I could take up residence again in the place where I belonged. That sense of being only a temporary resident had a profound effect on the way I lived for those years in that country. I simply could not bring myself to put down roots too deeply in a place that one day I would have to leave behind.

That mind-set, or attitude to life, comes out powerfully in the gallery of the faithful paraded before us in the book of Hebrews. It sets before us name after name of Old Testament saints, male and female, whose lives were

radically different from their faithless contemporaries and whose testimonies live on as an undying challenge to believers of subsequent generations. The nomadic lifestyle of Abraham and the generations which followed him becomes a kind of emblem of what it means to be a Christian. We see them always travelling with their gaze fixed on the horizon as they were looking for 'the city which has foundations whose builder and maker is God' (Heb. 11.10) which was to be found only in that 'better ... heavenly country' to which they were ultimately going (Heb. 11.16).

Their example and testimony have much to say to Christians living at this stage of human history, at least in the western world. Too many of God's people have become intoxicated by the materialistic mind-set which is almost universally characteristic of contemporary living. It has a dramatic effect on their spirituality and their effectiveness in living for God and serving him. The horizons of their life have become fixed in time and space, they live as though this world was all there was to be enjoyed and have lost that perspective on eternity future which transforms their view of life in the present. They desperately need a sight of heaven to which they can look forward.

Looking forward to rest

We can never be fully content with what we are and what we have here and now; we must live with a daily sense of anticipation of the best which is yet to be. As it was for Christian in Bunyan's well-known allegory, *Pilgrim's Progress*, the sight of the Celestial City on the horizon must fill us with a deep desire to reach our final destination

and there find the perfect rest for which our souls are longing. There alone is journey's end.

In the book of Hebrews, a letter addressed to believers for whom the tension and struggle of the life of faith were becoming a heavy burden, we read words of enormous comfort and encouragement: 'There remains therefore a rest for the people of God' (Heb. 4.9). Drawing on the great Old Testament theme of Sabbath rest and exploring it in the light of God's covenant promises to his people looking forward to the Promised Land, the writer demonstrates that the fullness of that promise can be experienced only in what God has prepared for his children in the age to come. His reference to the 'Today' of God's message to the world (Heb. 4.7) indicates that only a present response to what God offers in the gospel can allow a foretaste of these future blessings which will in eternity change from foretaste to full enjoyment. Anne Ross Cousin put it well in the words:

O Christ, he is the fountain,
The deep, sweet well of love;
The streams on earth I've tasted,
More deep I'll drink above;
There, to an ocean fulness,
His mercy doth expand,
And glory, glory dwelleth
In Immanuel's land.

The present joys of the Christian life are simply a realisation through faith today of what will be ours in perfection in God's eternal tomorrow. Thus being able to look forward to what that tomorrow has in store is of great importance for our present well-being.

The whole idea of total refreshment and spiritual as well as physical well-being tied up with the Sabbath principle in Scripture is crucial to our appreciation of the gospel. It is rest for the soul which Jesus promises to all who come to him (Matt. 11.28-30). That rest will only be found in heaven where the internal and external disruptions to life which are the consequence of sin finally will be removed. So when the apostle John gives us a glimpse of the heaven he saw in the Revelation, it is striking because of what is *not* there as much as because of what will be there. The absence of death, mourning, crying and pain immediately colours that new world-order in a way that is completely different from the 'old order of things which has passed away' (Rev. 21.4). Those intrusive enemies which rob people of peace and comfort in life will be banished for ever. But heaven will be no mere vacuum, its most striking characteristics will be those which have never been experienced on earth, at least not to the degree of perfection in which they will be found in the coming world.

There will be a newness to it all. Peter sees it as 'new heavens and new earth in which righteousness dwells' (2 Peter 3.13). Out of the ashes of the fallen world and universe whose very elements are doomed to be destroyed in a great heat (2 Peter 3.10), will arise a renovated world and universe.

It is vitally important for Christians to have this perspective on what will be theirs in eternity. The caricatured images of heaven – white-robed, long-faced, harp-toting, haloed people on clouds – are almost guaranteed to put people off the idea of heaven for life! Such images have arisen out of a literalistic understanding of descriptions of

heaven in the Bible which are meant to be seen as metaphor and simile, not the real thing. If we want to see heavenly realism, it is to Peter we must go, rather than the apocalyptic forms of Revelation. The down-to-earth former fisherman gives us a down-to-earth glimpse into what this new order will be like. It will be a world where we will feel totally at home.

There has perhaps been a tendency in popular evangelical understanding of heaven to emphasise its spiritual dimensions at the expense of the physical, to focus more on what theologians have called the 'intermediate state' instead of the 'eternal state'. That is, to dwell on the soul's being made perfect in holiness and passing into the immediate presence of Christ at death, rather than maintaining a balancing emphasis on the importance of the body and what is in store for it at the resurrection.[34] (This, incidentally, is why in a biblical understanding of the rites surrounding death, there will always be due care of and respect for the physical remains of the deceased, knowing that they still have a place in God's purpose for the individual who has departed.)

Most significantly it will enable Christians to hope for a heaven to which they can relate as spiritual and physical beings. There will be flowers to smell, mountains to climb, animals to enjoy, people to recognise and much more besides. Our resurrected bodies, like that of the resurrected Christ, will be perfectly equipped for life in that renewed and perfected environment (1 Cor. 15.12-14).

Of course, what makes home truly 'home' is not what it is like, but who is there. A house can have the most magnificent architecture, layout, decor and furnishings and

yet be a cavernous void if it is empty of someone to love. So with heaven, it will be the presence of Jesus himself who will turn it into Paradise. We have a faint glimpse of this during the Exodus when God threatened to withdraw his presence from his people and send them into the Promised Land without him (Exod. 33.1-16). When God issued this threat there was an amazing spontaneous expression of repentance on the part of the people and a plea from Moses: 'If your presence does not go with us, do not send us up from here' (Exod. 33.15). No matter if Canaan is 'a land flowing with milk and honey', bereft of God's presence, it might as well be Egypt or the wilderness.

Heaven could have all the wonders we could ever dream of, but if it did not have Jesus, it could never be home. Anne Ross Cousin again captured the sentiment of the true child of God:

> The bride eyes not her garment,
> But her dear Bridegroom's face;
> I will not gaze at glory,
> But on my King of grace;
> Not at the crown he giveth,
> But on his pierced hand;
> The Lamb is all the glory
> Of Immanuel's land.

It is indeed that Lamb who sits in the midst of the throne (Rev. 5.6) who provides the focus for John's graphic vision of what is to come. He will provide the 'fullness of joy and the pleasures for evermore' (Psalm 16.11) for those who are his own.

Discovering reality

It was the anticipation of his presence in heaven that Jesus highlighted for his disciples on earth as he prepared to leave them. As he reclined with them around the table in the Upper Room for the Last Supper, he told them he must leave them and he told them where he was going. Not only that, but he also explained why he was going away and why his departure should be a source of joy to them, not grief. In words that have been memorised by generations of Christians, Jesus says to his followers:

> Let not your hearts be troubled; you believe in God, believe also in Me. In My Father's house are many mansions; if it were not so, I would have told you. I go to prepare a place for you. And if I go and prepare a place for you, I will come again and receive you to Myself; that where I am, there you may be also (John 14.1-3).

That statement in itself must have been quite startling for the little band of Galileans who knew little or nothing about travel to distant places. The thought of a place for them, a place described as 'my Father's house' in which there were many rooms ('rooms' is a preferable translation to 'mansions') was incredibly exciting to contemplate. But the detail that was left ringing in their ears that night was the fact that their beloved Jesus would be there. His declared intention was to come back for them, take them to this place which he had made ready for them, then remain there with them for ever.

It is perhaps like the child going on holiday whose parents have gone into great detail describing where she

is going and what the accommodation is going to be like. She has been given a scintillating picture of what lies ahead. But the burning question in the child's mind with regard to her parents is, 'Will you be there?' The prospect of a holiday – even in the most exciting of locations – without the presence of parents, holds no attraction.

Thus the prospect of 'eternity with Jesus' forms the virtual epicentre of the Bible's teaching on heaven. That was the way in which the oldest convert in my last congregation described his conversion experience and the aspiration which lay at the heart of his new-found life in Christ. As a child he had been reared by loving Christian parents who set before him the truths about God's Son. As a young man he had turned his back upon that Jesus and the way of life associated with him. For a lifetime he had closed the door on God and everything Christian. But as an old man he could find no peace. For two years, he was later to tell me, he was tormented by the thought of spending eternity without Jesus. In the end, at the ripe old age of eighty two, he got down on his knees and, as he put it, 'begged the Lord to save him'. For the remaining years of his life he never tired of telling people how he came to be a child of God and would never fail to say that what he looked forward to more than anything else was, 'To spend eternity with Jesus'.

There are many aspects on life in heaven which the Bible is simply not clear about. This should not surprise us, because the sheer perfection of the place is too much for our finite, fallen minds to cope with – even Paul was overwhelmed by the glimpse God gave him of what lay ahead, and he was not allowed to tell of what he saw (2

Cor. 12.3-4). But one thing we can relate to and are encouraged to hold on to, is the fact that Jesus will be there. When John exults in the blessings of sonship, he looks forward to that eternal state and says:

> Beloved, now we are the children of God; and it has not yet been revealed what we shall be, but we know that when He is revealed, we shall be like Him, for we shall see Him as He is (1 John 3.2).

Our future in the family of God is bound up with Christ in a most extraordinary way. As we have been united to him through new birth and faith on earth and have begun to conform to his likeness as we are changed through grace, we can look forward to the day when that union ushers in perfect communion with him and perfect conformity to him as the pattern of true humanity.

This is the great reality that all need to discover. The words 'transient' and 'temporary' are written all over this world and all that it contains. The whole cosmos is in a state of steady decay. Even life itself is an inexorable journey from the cradle to the grave. In the words of James:

> For what is your life? It is even a vapour that appears for a little time and then vanishes away (James 4.14).

The Irish playwright, Samuel Beckett, was somewhat more cynical in the way he reflected on this reality. One of his characters musing on the brevity and futility of life stated:

> They give birth astride of a grave. The light gleams for an instant, then it's night once more.[35]

If we believe that this world and our all-too-brief experience of it is all there is, then we have failed to grasp the dimensions of life as it really is. If it is the case that even what we regard as the inanimate creation is actually longing for the return of God's Son and the consummation of God's plan (Rom. 8.19-22), then how much more do we, as thinking human beings who bear the image of the Creator, need to share the same desire.

There must be an ultimate home-coming, a day when the children of God are met at the door of their eternal home by the open arms of their Saviour and their Elder Brother, Jesus. There and then they will find the place for which their souls have longed.

> A tent or a cottage, why should I care?
> They're building a palace for me over there!
> Though exiled from home, yet still I may sing:
> All glory to God, I'm the child of a King!
>
> *I'm the child of a King, The child of a King!*
> *With Jesus my Saviour, I'm the child of a King!*

Epilogue

The issues we have explored in this book inevitably raise pertinent questions about ourselves and our own relationship with God. At the most basic level, as we begin to utter those familiar words of the Lord's Prayer, 'Our Father Who art in heaven...', we need urgently to ask if he is indeed *our* Father, as opposed to a vaguely known deity, remote from our experience. The urgency of the need to know God in this way is driven home by the exhortation we hear from Peter, when he says, 'Be even more diligent to make your calling and election sure' (2 Peter 1.10). We need to have certainty in life and there is none more important than a certainty about where we belong and where we will spend eternity.

It may well be that you do not know God in this way, that for you he is remote and unknown. Perhaps this is due in part to a failure to understand truly who he is and what it is he is calling you to in the gospel. For many people their impression of the Christian life is that of dull, ritualistic religion. That is all they have seen in the lives of those who claim to be Christians and that is all they have heard from those who claim to speak God's message. If that is so, then you would do well to think again in the light of the truths about God and his gospel that have been covered in these pages. Only then will we see God in all the warmth and attractiveness of his being and be encouraged to approach him in the grace offered through his Son.

The life he offers is the life we so desperately need and unwittingly yearn for. It has been Satan, the arch-enemy of our race, who has blinded our eyes to these realities. As Paul said to the Corinthians:

> ... the god of this world has blinded the minds of the unbelieving, that they might not see the light of the gospel of the glory of Christ, who is the image of God (2 Cor. 4.4, NASB).

The truth that we need to discover is the truth that God alone can reveal to us. It is that truth which will make us free.

The words by which Jesus directed his disciples towards heaven are the same words which direct us in to the most thrilling relationship we can ever know, one which brings us into fellowship with God. They are words which set God before us in the most intimate way in which he may be known. At one and the same time they show us the truth about the God who is love and the provision he has made through his one and only Son that people might come within his loving embrace. They set before us the crux of the issue in terms of where we stand in relation to God and how we think we can find favour with God. They are the words we need to take to heart and use as the litmus test of how we relate to him:

> I am the way, the truth and the life. No-one comes to *the Father*, except through me (John 14.6).

Have you come to trust that Saviour and through him received a place in God's family?

References

1. The three main contributions on the subject, each with slightly different emphases, were Robert S. Candlish, *The Fatherhood of God*, (A. & C. Black; Edinburgh) 1866; Thomas J. Crawford, *The Fatherhood of God* (William Blackwood & Sons; Edinburgh) 1867; John Kennedy, *Man's Relations to God* (Edinburgh: John Maclaren) 1869.

2. Reflected perhaps most notably by Sinclair B. Ferguson, *Children of the Living God* (Navpress; Colorado) 1987.

3. Robert S. Candlish, *The Fatherhood of God*.

4. John L. Girardeau, *Discussions of Theological Questions*, first published 1905, reprinted in 1986 (Sprinkle Publications; Harrisonburg Virginia) pp. 428-521.

5. *op cit* p.432

6. *Westminster Shorter Catechism* Question 34

7. *Westminster Shorter Catechism* Question 104

8. A point argued more fully by Wayne Grudem, *Systematic Theology* (IVP: Leicester) 1994 p.737.

9. Some scholars wish to push the dating of *Galatians* back as far as AD 48-49, see discussion in, Hiebert, E.D., *An Introduction to the New Testament: Volume 2*, pp. 82-88 (Moody Press; Chicago) 1977.

10. So the NASB

11. So the NIV

12. *The Westminster Shorter Catechism* Answer 22

13. See chapter 1

14. See G.C. Berkouwer's discussion of 'Justification from Eternity' in *Faith and Justification* (W.B. Eerdmans; Grand Rapids) 1977, pp. 143-168.

15. 'Glory of the Father' is a better reading than 'Glory of God', so, NASB and NIV.

16. See, e.g., C.E.B. Cranfield, *Romans* Volume 1, International Critical Commentary Series (T&T Clark, Edinburgh) 1982, pp.304-305.

17. This was the Authorised Version's rendering of the Greek word *parakletos* (John 14:16, 26; 16:7), which, while not fully doing justice to this title given to the Spirit, nevertheless well expresses something of his function.

18. *Westminster Confession of Faith*, Chapter 12, Of Adoption

19. *ibid*

20. See also pages 67, 68, 71

21. For a fuller treatment of this see, Meredith G. Kline, *The Structure of Biblical Authority* (W.B. Eerdmans; Grand Rapids, Michigan) 1981.

22. This frequently overlooked Old Testament theme is well explored by Tremper Longman and Daniel G. Reid in, *God is a Warrior* (Paternoster; Carlisle UK) 1995.

23. NKJV Margin

24. See Chris Wright, *Living as the People of God* (IVP; Leicester) 1983, pp. 46-66.

25. *The Westminster Shorter Catechism* Q. 7

26. The punctuation of the NKJV obscures the fact that it was 'in love' that God predestined his children.

27. See Sinclair Ferguson's discussion of the Spirit as 'seal' in *The Holy Spirit* (IVP; Leicester) 1996 pp. 180-182.

28. *The Westminster Shorter Catechism* Q. 43-44; *The Westminster Larger Catechism* Q.101-102

29. *The Westminster Confession of Faith* 8.1

30. *idem*

31. See especially the literature associated with the American Church Growth Movement.

32. See Geoffrey Hanks, *60 Great Founders* (Christian Focus Publications) 1995.

33. See Introduction.

34. *The Westminster Shorter Catechism* Q.37 preserves the balance perfectly.

35. Samuel Beckett, *Waiting for Godot*, Act 2.

Focus on Faith is a series of books designed to explain the important doctrines of the faith. In addition to *Child of a King* by Mark Johnston other titles in the series available in 1997 will include

The New Birth by Andrew T.B. MacGowan
Andrew MacGowan is Director of the Highland Theological Institute, Elgin, Scotland where he teaches theology and church history. In his book he considers the meaning of the doctrine of regeneration and where it fits in the order of salvation.

Our God is Awesome by Ken M. Campbell
Ken Campbell is Associate Professor of Biblical Studies at Belhaven College, Jackson, Mississippi, USA. This book explains in a meaningful way the attributes of God.

Baptism by Rodger Crooks
Rodger Crooks is minister of Belvoir Presbyterian Church, Belfast, Northern Ireland. His book presents the biblical and historical case for the validity of infant baptism.

Other titles will be added to the series in the future.

SELECTED INDEX

SCRIPTURE INDEX

188

190

Colossians
1:15 76
1:17 70
2:9 42, 139
3:2 109

Philippians
1:6 129
1:21 142
1:21-23 169
2:7 42
3:4-6 141
3:8 141, 142
3:9 169
3:10-11 169
3:12 169
3:13-14 142
3:14-15 169
3:20 168

1 Timothy
2:5 43

2 Timothy
1:12 122
2:11-13 128
3:16 108

Hebrews
1:1-3 42
2:10 31
2:11 66
2:11-12 65
2:14 42
2:17 42, 67
4:13 28
4:15 42, 72
4:16 72, 98
4:7 173
4:9 173
5:1 68
10:22 98
10:23 152
10:24 153
11:6 49
11:10 172
11:16 172
12:1-3 48, 144
12:2 144
12:5-8 112
12:9-11 113
12:14 113

James
1:17 114
4:14 179
5:19-20 159

1 Peter
1:1 171
1:2 55
1:22 153

2 Peter
1:4 86
1:10 181
3:10 174
3:13 174

1 John
1:5 137
1:9 129
1:10 160
2:19 126
3:1 45, 62
3:1-2 58
3:2 45, 62, 179
3:3 59
3:14 133
4:8 51
4:10 55, 56
4:19 136

Revelation
5:6 176
13:8 73
21:4 174

D1497609

Mark Johnston has been minister of Grove Chapel, London since 1994. Prior to that, he was pastor of the Evangelical Presbyterian Church in Richhill in Northern Ireland. His theological studies included several years at Westminster Theological Seminary in Philadelpia, USA. Mark is married with two children. His interests include fishing and photography. His published works include contributing several articles to the NIV Thematic Bible (published by Hodder & Stoughton) and a chapter in the book entitled *Gender and Leadership* (Day One Publications).